PAUL AND THE ROMANS

Denise L.
Stringer

PAUL and the ROMANS

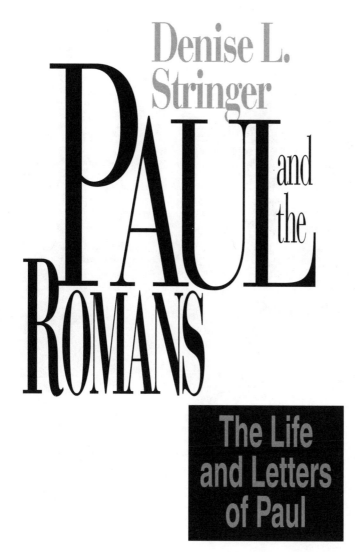

The Life and Letters of Paul

Abingdon Press
Nashville

PAUL AND THE ROMANS

This book is printed on acid-free paper.

ISBN 0-687-09079-2

03 04 05 06 07 08 09 — 10 9 8 7 6 5 4 3

Manufactured in the United States of America

CONTENTS

HOW TO USE
THIS RESOURCE

Welcome to *Paul and the Romans*, a seven-session study on Paul's letter and his relationship with the Roman congregations. Each of the seven chapters contains common elements designed to help you use this resource successfully in a group setting or as a personal study.

"Read Romans"

First you will note throughout each chapter that there are a number of subheadings that direct you to read a portion of Romans. While there may also be cross references to numerous other passages in the Bible, the Romans passage is the key to the lesson. If this is an individual endeavor, you can read the Bible references as you encounter them.

Convenient Short Blocks of Text

Second you will find that the subheadings break up text into segments that are usually about two-to-three pages long. While the information in the chapter forms a coherent whole, the ideas are "sized" so that you can not only take the long view but also spend time with distinct ideas within the whole.

Study Questions

At the end of each of these divisions within the chapter are study and discussion questions that relate to that segment of the text. Many of the questions are designed to make sure you understand the biblical text. Romans is a complicated piece of Scripture, and the apostle's argument may sound foreign or confusing to 21st-century culture.

Other questions are more analytical and ask readers to assess meanings for the original audience. That understanding leads to another level of study helps: personal reflection on what the revealed meaning of the biblical passage means and how those learnings and faithful insights can be applied to one's life.

Closing

At the end of each chapter are some suggestions for closing that apply to both a group and an individual setting. Many times you will be asked to summarize the content and import of that chapter and the selected Scripture. In each instance, you are invited to a time of prayer.

Leading a Group

If you are leading a group, these pointers will help you plan the study session:

• Read the entire chapter, including all the Scriptures.
• Think about your group members: their needs, their experience with the Bible and with each other, their questions. From this information, establish one or two session goals.

- Pay particular attention to the study questions and select at least one or two questions, if possible, from each segment of the text. Keeping in mind your group and your goals, note which questions you intend to cover. Try to have a variety of content, analytical, and personal application questions and activities.
- Encourage group members to use their Bibles and to read these texts.
- Be comfortable with silence and give group members a chance to think. Be sure that no one dominates and that everyone has the opportunity to participate.
- Have an intentional closure to the session by engaging in the suggested prayer or other spiritual discipline.
- Accept our best wishes and blessings for a transformational and edifying study time.

I THE APOSTOLIC MINISTRY OF PAUL

The Gift of Apostleship

P aul, the man who wrote the single most influential first-century letter, understood himself to be an apostle to the non-Jewish world. He believed that Jesus of Nazareth, risen and empowered to bring about God's reign on earth, commissioned him to be the chief witness for his gospel beyond Palestine, throughout the Roman Empire, and on to Spain via Rome. As Paul prepared to visit with the Christians in Rome, he wanted to establish a relationship of mutual understanding and fellowship with the established ministry there, to encourage the believers toward unity, and to correct any misunderstandings that might have existed relative to his teaching. *with money* He hoped that the church at Rome would sponsor him in his mission to Spain, once it became thoroughly acquainted with his gospel and his calling from Christ. Therefore he composed a lengthy epistle, with the probable intent that it would be read in at least three house churches in various neighborhoods of the capital city.

Paul believed his ministry to be a gift from God. Although he had an excellent background in the study of the Hebrew Scriptures and Greek rhetoric, spoke both Aramaic (the language of the Hebrews) and Greek, and had lived in both Israel and in Greek parts of the Roman

Empire, it was not only his many qualifications for the Gentile mission that equipped him to serve. Education and expertise would not have sufficed as background and training for the colossal task of spreading the gospel in a pagan culture. Moreover, Paul, as a devout Jew, could never have comprehended the mystery of the gospel or communicated its power for salvation. Only the gracious experience of seeing the Lord could have prepared him. Only a personal, ongoing relationship of faith in Christ could have sustained Paul in the face of all the obstacles and persecution he would encounter.

Paul received the gospel through a revelation of Jesus Christ (Galatians 1:11-12; compare Acts 9:3-6). The term *revelation* refers to a visual experience provided by God whereby the recipient "sees" some truth that could not be comprehended or experienced otherwise. It was in this sense that Saul (or Paul) of Tarsus, a zealous Jew, became an "eyewitness" to the Resurrection (1 Corinthians 15:8-10).

Sometimes the visual dimension of a revelation is augmented by an audition or by an impression of a verbal communication. In any case, the revelation must be interpreted in order to become effective. Paul says that he learned the gospel by way of his extraordinary experience. The message that he preached tirelessly and productively, probably from about A.D. 33 until his death in the early 60's, he originally received directly from the risen Christ (Galatians 1:15-17).

Not only did Paul receive the gift of faith in Christ and the message he was to spread to the Gentiles through this revelation, he also experienced grace for himself. Paul, according to his own testimony, had personally and vigorously opposed God's saving purpose in Jesus' death and resurrection (Galatians 1:13). He had harassed the earliest

Christians. He very possibly had overseen the torture and death of some, probably including that of Stephen (Acts 7:54–8:1). In all this, Paul had felt justified and even proud of himself until he "saw the Lord . . . high and lofty," as Isaiah the prophet had so long before (Isaiah 6:1-8). Now he felt profound guilt and deep shame for this insubordination to and betrayal of God. Paul believed that he deserved to die. Instead of condemnation, however, he experienced forgiveness and reconciliation. He became a changed man. This was the essential Christian experience at work: faith in God's forgiveness granted through Jesus Christ, leading to a change of heart, mind, lifestyle, and identity.

THE GIFT OF APOSTLESHIP

• How did Paul become convicted in his Christian faith?
• What is the essence of the Christian faith experience for you?
• Recall how you first came to believe. In what sense is your faith a gift from God?

Paul's Religious History
Read Romans 15:14-21, 30-33

Paul, the Pharisee, died to his former self-understanding and sense of purpose and rose into a new life, illumined by his visionary experience. In order to appreciate the reformation in his theology and religious practice, as well as to understand its roots, it is helpful to be conscious of some of the most salient beliefs that shaped the apostle's earlier thought.

Paul was a Pharisee. This prominent party within Judaism believed in the bodily resurrection of the dead. The Pharisees expected a literal opening of the graves to take place at the end of history, upon the coming of a mes-

siah. Through this heavenly male figure, God would judge
the living and the dead and establish God's reign, having
defeated Satan, sin, and death. As a Pharisee, Paul
embraced the widely held Jewish apocalyptic view of history, as did most first-century Jews and others similarly
oppressed and despairing of the human condition.

Like all good Jews, moreover, the Pharisees believed
that the study and observance of Scripture was the highest
vocation and deepest virtue. In their zeal to honor the
Torah, they adhered strictly to purity laws. These rules of
conduct and religious ritual were designed to protect the
faithful from the risk of disobeying the demands and
intentions of the Ten Commandments as well as to maintain readiness for worship. The purity laws were complex
and demanding, most notably those that related to diet.
The keeping of them separated the devout from the casual
or less-observant Jew and sometimes led to pride, prejudice, exclusion, and division.

The most rigorously devout likely experienced a certain
level of anxiety over adequately observing these many reg-
ulations. This may have led, in some cases, to hyper-vigi-
lance. The devout were known to seek assurance of their
salvation directly from God, fearing that their observance
of the law might be less than perfect. According to Howard
Clark Kee, writing in *Christianity* (Macmillan Publishing
Company, 1991), some received this assurance in the form
of a mystical experience through which they were taken by
the Spirit into the throne room of God.[1] Paul apparently
had this high privilege (2 Corinthians 12:1-7a).

So powerful was the memory of that vision that it moti-
vated Paul to overcome the great odds against the success
of his work (2 Corinthians 11:23-33) and continually
guided his thinking and teaching as a religious prophet

and innovator. Note his determination in the midst of anxiety in preparing to return to Jerusalem with an offering for the believers there (Romans 15:30-32). Paul's ministry challenged the doctrine and practice of the first-century synagogue to the extent that his most serious opposition came from among his fellow Jews.

In summary, Paul's worldview and experience as a Pharisee shaped the way he interpreted the revelation he received. It confirmed his belief in bodily resurrection and intensified his expectation that the Messiah would soon come to judge the world. It determined the pattern of his teaching style, causing him to refer to Hebrew Scripture to prove the validity of his argument. And it prepared him to provide his converts with practical ethical instruction as the rabbis before him had. Nevertheless, that revelation profoundly refocused his thinking and self-understanding, causing his teaching and preaching to distinguish the gospel from the Law in a radical way. Paul's ministry was informed by his conversion and call. That early revelation functioned as the defining moment of his life and as the means by which he interpreted all history. It forged the core of his spiritual life and was the essence of his charisma.

PAUL'S RELIGIOUS HISTORY

• Review Romans 15:14-21, 30-33. How did Paul view his calling and ministry? How did he present himself and this ministry to the congregation at Rome?

• Look up 2 Corinthians 11:23-33. Paul's former life as a Jew was transformed by his call by Jesus Christ. How would you describe the discontinuity and the continuity between Paul's Jewish faith and his Christian beliefs and practice? *Law*

• Reflect on your own faith journey and any major shifts you may have experienced in the way you perceive reality. Was your conversion gradual, dramatic, or is it still in process? Have you had any vivid moments of revelation? If so, how do you interpret them? *Unexpected*

Paul's Call to Ministry:
His Message, His Goal, His Vocation
Read Romans 1:1-15

Paul's conversion and call to ministry occurred as one physically and emotionally charged experience. He nevertheless formulated a clear statement of his sense of mandate and of what he had come to know from his encounter with the risen Christ. One of the many places in which he recorded a simple statement of the gospel may be found in his greeting to the church at Rome. In that greeting Paul asserts that Jesus was a Jew of the lineage of the Jewish King David to whom God had promised a perpetual reign. Jesus' resurrection from the dead to reign as Lord over all creation fulfilled God's promise to David. Jesus is the Son of God, as made plain and effective by God's raising him from the dead. Those who affirm the salvation made available through Jesus and who confess him as Lord live in a right relationship with God by faith, apart from any religious duty or legal requirements. In this, God proves God's own goodness by providing both a means of release from the condemnation all deserve because of sin and a means for upright living. The goal of it all, both for God and for Paul, was nothing new: to bring about "the obedience of faith" for all (1:5-6).

Out of this obedience of faith, Paul became "a servant of Jesus Christ" (1:1). There was no choice for him. Paul belonged to God and could only find meaning and fulfillment by working with God toward the salvation of the world. Paul's part was to reach the Gentile world and to lead the churches under his care to support that work.

In fulfilling his vocation, Paul had become a missionary evangelist. He preached the gospel, generally where others had not preceded him, founding churches and turning them over to pastors, administrators, and teachers whom he had either trained or approved. Paul served as mentor and supervised the work of many ministers of the gospel and worked diligently to care for the spiritual life of his congregations by exhorting them, resolving disputes, refuting heresies, providing ethical and other practical advice, and praying fervently for his converts.

Paul assumed that the Christians in Rome knew, as he did, that God had called them to a life of holiness. They were to be saints; that is, they were to be people utterly dedicated to the honor and service of God (1:7). Therein lay their joy and their peace. Nevertheless, as the apostle to the Gentiles, he felt compelled to take some responsibility for the sanctity of the congregational life in Rome, as he had in the other Gentile cities, even though he had not founded the congregations there (15:14-16).

As a witness to the resurrection of Jesus and his authority as Lord, Paul's apostolic work required his best talent and his total dedication. Paul expected a similar level of dedication from his fellow Christians in Rome. Specifically, he expected that the Roman Christians would want to provide financial assistance to the further work of the gospel that Paul hoped to undertake in Spain. He was sending Phoebe, a deacon and his financial patron, ahead of him to prepare the way for his visit. Luke Timothy Johnson, in his work *Reading Romans: A Literary and Theological Commentary,* calls her Paul's "financial agent" (page 217).[2] Paul expected the church at Rome to welcome her as they would him, showing her generous hospitality and cooperating with her in every way that she required (Romans 16:1-2). In this way the church at Rome would share in Paul's apostolic ministry and assist him in fulfilling his God-given vocation.

PAUL'S CALL TO MINISTRY

• Read Romans 1:3-6. What was the gospel as Paul preached it? How do you understand the concept of obedience in this passage? How did Paul expect the Roman congregation to demonstrate this obedience?
• To what extent do you consider yourself a slave or servant of Christ? To what extent, then, do you feel God calls you to a life of complete dedication? Find a contemporary metaphor to describe total dedication to God's work. *Mother Theresa*

vs

Ultra conservative or cult-like liberalism

A Strategy for Mission
Read Romans 16:1-16, 21-24

Paul's success in establishing lasting mission congregations in numerous cities throughout Asia Minor and Greece deserves study, inasmuch as the conditions under which he worked to spread the gospel are in many ways similar to those of the church in North America. The Roman Empire was a pluralistic society. Its cities hosted diverse religious and ethnic groups living together in densely settled neighborhoods. Because of the relatively advanced system of roads connecting Rome to all its territories and protectorates, most notably the Via Egnatia and the Appian Way, the people traveled freely and easily, taking with them their beliefs, customs, and news. Safer travel by sea, due to the government's success in controlling piracy, allowed for the influx of culture, products, and emigrants from the East. Communication among regions, enhanced by the widespread use of Greek as the language of commerce and by the Roman postal system, took days rather than months. The economy was strong, and the region enjoyed nearly a century of freedom from war. The leisure, wealth, and travel afforded by the *pax romana* fostered moral laxity at all levels of society.

Finally, the first century A.D. was a period of religious searching. The population demonstrated a high level of interest in spiritual matters. Religious freedom typified the period, allowing for exploration of a wide range of rituals and ideologies, as well as the growth of Jewish communities throughout the Empire, especially in Rome. In all these ways, the Roman Empire of Paul's day operated much like our own society in the twenty-first century. If we are to be effective in spreading the gospel in the new millennium, we must learn from Paul.

Paul was an itinerant. He traveled mostly on foot, though also by sea, without significant possessions. He apparently had no home of his own or any strong kinship ties. We know of Paul's nephew from Acts 23:16-22, but for the most part Paul's family seemed to be the church. His support network came from his coworkers and from the congregations he founded. His emotional home was the fellowship of believers.

Paul had been authorized and sent to carry out his mission by the apostles at Jerusalem (Galatians 2:1-10). Although Paul's vision and understanding came directly by revelation, his authorization to pursue his calling came from the church. The congregation at Antioch, where he and Barnabas had shared an extended ministry, may have initiated the outreach to Asia Minor (Acts 13:1-3). Paul gained from the church certification of orthodoxy for his teaching, the affirmation of the Holy Spirit speaking through other Christian prophets, and a partner in ministry.

Paul never worked alone. He took companions with him for fellowship and for the extension and reinforcement of his work (Romans 16:1-16, 21-24; Galatians 2:1). The congregation at Philippi became his chief benefactor,

providing financial support and also personal care through
Epaphroditus, one of their members (Philippians 4:15-18).

Paul began his missionary work in each new area by
establishing a base of operations in a major city. These
cities included Ephesus in Asia, Thessalonica in
Macedonia, Corinth in Achaia, and Rome while he was
in prison there. Since Paul was what Wayne Meeks called
an urban "artisan" in his book entitled *The First Urban
Christians* (page 9),[3] Paul more than likely started working
with his hands among his fellow tradespersons and built a
fellowship through those connections. Someone among his
coworkers who had a larger than average apartment
would open his or her home to a group gathered to hear
Paul speak. A congregation composed of people with similar backgrounds and interests would develop in that person's home.

Extended families often provided the nucleus of these
house churches. The nuclear family would often live in
proximity to other kin, servants, and employees. This network of people would be naturally drawn into contact
with Paul the missionary. Word of the meetings spread
quickly and easily in an urban environment by way of
family members, coworkers, and neighbors speaking to
one another on the street. The format of the house church
was not unlike that of the religious clubs and trade guilds
common throughout the cities of the Roman Empire.

It is entirely possible, as Luke reports, that Paul would
also teach in the synagogues on the sabbath until resistance emerged (Acts 18:4-5). The Jewish synagogues
would be host not only to Jews but also to "God-fearers,"
that is, persons who converted to monotheism and were
sympathetic to Jewish practice. This sector of the Jewish
congregation would have been the group most likely to

Parallel to persons today seeking a congregation (involvement) rather than a denomination)

21

respond favorably to Paul's message. They were seekers after God who did not have strong ties to the Hebrew tradition.

This multi-dimensional approach served Paul well in the years preceding his visit to Rome. He anticipated continuing his strategy in Spain after gaining the support of the congregations in Rome. While in Rome, he hoped to meet with each of the house churches there and, no doubt, with the Jews on the sabbath. Although his purpose in Rome was not to found a new church, his strategy for communicating the gospel and making converts in that pagan metropolis would follow a similar pattern.

PAUL'S STRATEGY FOR MINISTRY

• What similarities do you see between the Roman Empire in Paul's day and your own context for ministry? *C85*
• Read Romans 16:1-16, 21-24 and note the way in which Paul mentioned fellow Christians as his family. What does that suggest about his support and strategy for building up the congregation?
• Read Acts 13:1-3, Galatians 2:1-10, and Philippians 4:15-18. What strategies for ministry do you see demonstrated there?
• What aspects of Paul's mission strategy might apply to reaching people with the gospel and fostering new congregations in your area?

Mission churches

The Congregations in Rome and Their Context for Ministry

Research suggests that three house churches existed in Rome at the time of Paul's writing to them from Corinth. These house churches were composed of Gentile Christians, living in what had been the Jewish quarter, the section of the city where immigrants from throughout the Empire first settled.

These congregations, whether Gentile or Jewish, were largely composed of slaves, former slaves, laborers, and artisans like Prisca and Aquila. The Christians were a small minority group within a large urban culture. Their numbers may have been as low as one hundred at the time Paul wrote. Due to the history of religious persecution under Claudius, it was important that they learn to live in harmony with the government and the military officials (Romans 13:1-7).

The major cities of Paul's world, including Rome, were "affluent, cosmopolitan, pluralistic, and more than a little libertine," according to Peter Berger writing for the journal *First Things* in 1990.[4] The religious milieu included cults of magic, the worship of the emperor as savior, mystery religions, and cults of healing—most involving idols in their religious observances and some featuring temple prostitution. The citizens who followed these various cults and sects were reaching out to the gods to align their lives with them and to find meaning.[5] At the same time, a revival of philosophy—Platonic, Aristotelian, and Stoic—was underway. This urban center, the capital city of the Empire, had only begun to be evangelized. The Roman Empire dominated the entire career of the early church. Paul's influence from Rome would come to color his influence in the churches there. Ultimately the church in Rome became one of the most significant foci of Christianity in the world.

THE CONGREGATIONS IN ROME

• Compare the house churches of Rome with the small groups in your church. What might make your small groups more effective in reaching, including, and nurturing new disciples of Christ?

Margin notes:
Common persona
Not elite *
upper class

(from women's role as "mother earth" God: fulfillment)
Religion ceremony prostitution

Check "joy" passage
Romans 15:24-27

CB'?

balance "growth" with "recruitment"
Example is the best influence

Conservative WASP

• What is the religious landscape of your community? Whom do you know who does not actively participate in a Christian congregation (and is not a member of a non-Christian tradition)? What, if anything, are they doing to explore their spirituality? How might you reach out to them with the gospel?

Conservative WASP

• What is the social, economic, and ethnic makeup of your congregation? of your office or school? of your community? How does that diversity, or lack of diversity, enhance your life? your worship life? your social life? How can you reach out in culturally sensitive ways to spread the gospel? *informs reality*

IN CLOSING

• Review your learning about the nature of apostleship and of the strategies of spreading the gospel. What are your main insights from the Scriptures and the text? Then review how these insights help you grow in your own sense of apostleship: of one who is sent as a representative of Jesus Christ.
• Close with prayer for all those who labor in God's work, such as church professionals, and for those who see their labor as God's work, regardless of profession.

---

[1] From "The Context, Birth, and Early Growth of Christianity," by Howard Clark Kee, in *Christianity*, by Howard Clark Kee, Emily Albu Hanawalt, Carter Lindberg, Jean-Loup Seban, and Mark A. Noll (Macmillan Publishing Company, 1991); pages 11–143.

[2] From *Reading Romans: A Literary and Theological Commentary*, by Luke Timothy Johnson (The Crossroad Publishing Company, 1997); page 217.

[3] From *The First Urban Christians*, by Wayne A. Meeks (Yale University Press, 1983); page 9.

[4] From "Worldly Wisdom, Christian Foolishness," by Peter L. Berger, in *First Things* (June/July 1990); page 16.

[5] From *The Writings of St. Paul*, edited by Wayne A. Meeks (W.W. Norton & Company, Inc., 1972).

II ESTABLISHING COMMON GROUND: THE UNIVERSAL NEED FOR SALVATION

Introduction to the Body of the Letter
Read Romans 1:1-17

The greeting section of the Letter to the Romans (Romans 1:1-17) functions as an introduction of the apostle to his readers and as a statement of his purpose in writing (1:1-6). It includes a salutation, found in verse 7. A prayer of thanksgiving for the Christians of Rome follows in verses 8-15. Verses 16-17 serve as Paul's thesis statement.

In seeking to understand any document, a careful study of the thesis leads to greater comprehension of the entire piece. In attempting to understand Paul's thesis, it may help to consider a paraphrase. Paul takes the position that the gospel is the dynamic Word of God. This Word is effective for the salvation of all people who receive it in an attitude of submission to the divine authority and truth it represents. The gospel belongs first to the Jews, but then to everyone else. Through the gospel, God demonstrates God's goodness and fairness. Those who receive this revelation by faith enter into a right relationship with God, self, and neighbor. The body of Paul's letter to the church at Rome, Chapters 1–11, develops the thesis in light of his relationship with the people he describes in his salutation and thanksgiving and in light of his apostolic vocation.

Over the centuries since Paul first wrote this letter, theologians, biblical scholars, pastors, teachers, and laypersons have frequently thought of Romans as the closest thing to systematic theology available in the New Testament. Some people have used it as a source of Christian doctrine. Many have found profound power for personal transformation in reading the letter, as if it were addressed to individuals seeking a right relationship with God rather than to the corporate church. What, though, was Paul's intent in structuring his material as he did and in using the particular teaching devices he chose?

Several factors must have contributed to the way Paul ultimately presented his gospel. According to noted Bible scholar Luke Timothy Johnson, Paul wrote from Corinth during the winter months of A.D. 57–58, as indicated by the greetings from Erastus, the city treasurer there (Romans 16:23). Paul was on his way to Jerusalem with the collection for the mother church and was anticipating a conflict that had been developing there for some time. Jewish Christians in several cities where Paul had worked had accused him of saying that no Christian should be circumcised or otherwise practice Jewish tradition.

The intensity of this controversy may have been heightened by Paul's exhortation to the Galatians on the subject of circumcision (Galatians 3:1-5). Before going to Rome to present his credentials for mission, he wanted to make it clear that he was a Jew who respected the practices of his fellow Jewish Christians in not only keeping the Law but also in fulfilling it! Moreover, he wanted to assert his own deep love for his kinsmen, his fellow Jews (see, for example, Galatians 2:1-10). He hoped to correct any false impressions of his own viewpoint and to encourage a similar attitude of mutual respect in the midst of diversity at

Rome. Paul took care, therefore, to present the gospel with frequent reference to its origins in the Hebrew tradition, drawing on the Torah, the Prophets, and the Writings. Because this concern to clarify his position was not only a matter of religious tolerance but also one of theology, Paul developed his letter around the question of the nature of God as revealed in Jesus' death and resurrection. The body of the letter is, therefore, rightly understood as theological in its argumentation.

Paul's thinking about God assumes several things as common ground between Paul and his audience. First, they all believed in one God who created the world and everyone in it. Second, they all believed this God to be just, that is, impartial and demanding obedience to God's authority. Third, they agreed that the Torah makes plain what God requires. Those who know it are accountable to God for their behavior in light of that law. Fourth, both Paul and the church he addressed trusted that God's purpose in history is aimed at the salvation of the world, which will come about over time and will break the power of sin that holds humanity in its grasp. These concepts were widely agreed upon in first-century Judaism as well as within the Christian community. Nevertheless, many people behaved as if these points were not true.

Paul's theological purpose was, therefore, not merely academic. It was oriented toward bringing his readers into full submission to the truth, not as a matter of duty or intellectual assent, but by way of the power of salvation at work in them through the Spirit. Paul was more an evangelist than he was a scholar. While he used all available tools of rhetoric and his best powers of reason, he sought to engage the souls of the believers in the truth for their transformation (Romans 12:1-2).

Paul developed his thesis in a strategic manner. He first established the universal need for salvation. He then answered that need with the gospel of the crucified and risen Lord, established the terms by which salvation may be gained, and described the new life that unfolds for those who are being saved. This salvation results in "life in Christ" or "life in the Spirit," so Paul devoted considerable attention to the nature of Christian spirituality. Having reached the climax of his message, he then turned to the subject of the salvation of the Jewish people as a matter related to the sovereignty of God.

Having acknowledged the mystery and the glory of God's saving purpose, Paul then dealt with the practical implications of the new life. As he stated in his original greeting, his purpose was to encourage and nurture Gentiles in the obedience of faith, not only by acknowledging God and God's saving act, but also by entering into a life of righteousness. The final section of the letter (Romans 12–16) is more personal and functional than theological and thus should not be considered a part of the body of the letter.

The voice with which Paul addressed the Christians at Rome is markedly different from the voice heard in his letters to other Christian communities. His tone, for example, in the letters to the Thessalonians is encouraging and instructive. He wrote to the Philippians with fond intimacy. His letters to the Corinthians might be described as directive and assertive. His voice in writing to the Galatians could be considered aggressive. None of these dimensions of Paul's relationship with his congregations will be felt in a reading of the Letter to the Romans. Instead, Paul seems more humble, or at least, less self-assertive in this letter (1:11-12).

Paul wrote, not as a superintendent of the work at Rome or as a pastor, but as a missionary evangelist seeking the support and fellowship of his fellow believers. Paul's standing with Rome was tenuous; therefore, he could not exhort them directly, but apparently felt a need to earn the right to provide pastoral guidance by building trust and a theological context for his ministry with them. He approached his practical concerns with great dexterity, avoiding potential alienation and hoping to encourage relationships of joyful harmony among people whom he, for the most part, did not yet know.

INTRODUCTION TO THE BODY OF THE LETTER

• Read Romans 1:16-17. Restate Paul's thesis as you understand it.
• Read Romans 1:1-6. How does Paul introduce his belief and what he hopes to accomplish? How does he establish his "credentials"? How might this introduction have struck you if you were among the congregation?
• Read Romans 1:8-15. Paul takes a much less self-assertive stand in presenting himself to the Romans than he does in some of his letters to other congregations. If he were writing to you, how would you have been inclined to receive him? to identify with his goals?
• What is the common ground that Paul shared with the Roman congregation? Do you agree with each of these four assumptions? Explain.

Natural Revelation, Conscience, and the Creator
Read Romans 1:18-32

Creation itself makes the nature of God plainly visible, Paul asserts. Nevertheless, people choose to disregard God and to rebel against what good conscience dictates. As a result, they lose their power to think responsibly and productively. They think they are more sophisticated than those who submit to God's authority; but, in fact, they

prove how corrupt and confused they really are. By giving
their devotion to things that are not God and defying the
very nature of God, they pave the way for their own
destruction. God condemns their idolatry and immorality.
In fact, Paul asserts that the "wrath of God is revealed
from heaven against all ungodliness and wickedness of
those who by their wickedness suppress the truth"
(Romans 1:18). When Paul used such vivid language
about God, he was not so much describing an angry despot as he was seeking to claim the attention of his readers
regarding the ultimate significance and entirely natural
consequences of self-destructive behavior.

Paul described the general human condition by writing,
"They exchanged the truth about God for a lie and worshiped and served the creature rather than the Creator"
(1:25). This is Paul's timeless assertion against the folly of
yielding our souls to anything other than the source of our
life, who is God. When we do, we see the signs of God's
wrath (1:24-31). Sin is, at its core, in Paul's view, a failure
to acknowledge one's dependence on God, resulting in
insubordination to God's authority and service to something less than God. Paul assumed, as Jesus did, that all
people serve something or someone (Luke 16:13). Paul
believed, without hesitation, that all of creation depends on
God for its very existence, let alone its integrity. Paul found
it appalling that anyone would deny this or risk losing sight
of this fact. Even worse, he felt, was the state of those who
organized their lives around a focus on something material
and inanimate or around their own appetites. He illustrated
his point by reporting the obscene sexual practices to
which lust leads people (Romans 1:26-27).

Paul's choice of illustration has provided fertile soil for
controversy in recent years. The original Greek composi-

Homosexuality

tion of verse 26 does not automatically support the almost universal assumption that Paul here refers to lesbian sexual acts. There is very little comment on this type of practice, though it was acknowledged in Greek literature and history. There is, however, some written indication, according to James E. Miller writing for *Novum Testamentum* (Volume 37, 1995), that women would engage in "unnatural" (that is, non-coital) sexual activity as prostitutes or adulteresses in order to attract and keep lovers or to avoid pregnancy, all practices that Paul would condemn.[1]

The reference in verse 27 to sexual activity between two men does have extra-biblical support. Pederasty, a practice in which a man uses a boy for sexual gratification (purportedly to teach the boy about his own sexuality), was common in the Hellenistic period. Because all men married unless they were physically or mentally unable to do so, we can assume that this practice of pederasty involved what many would consider a form of adultery. The young man so treated was likewise considered unmarriageable (or perhaps as "damaged goods"). His compromised status could, and often did, lead him into male prostitution, which was neither uncommon nor approved of. He may also have been so led to assume the role of pederast as an adult and thus perpetuate the practice. One of the emperors is reported to have had a male lover (which was homosexual, not pederastic, behavior). Homosexual practices were known in the first century, but not as monogamous relationships. Paul, like all Jews, found these practices heinous and self-destructive.

Paul further illustrated the results of rebellion against God by compiling a list of common vices (Romans 1:28-32). Note that his list has nothing to do with private sin, such as pride or prejudice. Each vice adversely affects relationships.

Likely Paul's choice of vices, from among all those that had been listed by a variety of religious and philosophical teachers of the age, reflects Paul's emphasis on love of neighbor as the just requirement of the Law (13:8). He also cautions against judgment. While behavior destructive to the community (1:29-31) must be challenged, all are immersed enough in their own sin and dare not judge (2:1).

NATURAL REVELATION, CONSCIENCE, AND THE CREATOR

• Using a Bible dictionary or the notes in your study Bible, define the "wrath of God." What does that mean in the context of Romans 1:18-32?

• Romans 1:24-25 summarizes Paul's understanding of sin: that deep alienation from God that occurs when humankind loses sight of their status as creature and elevates anything over the Creator. Is that definition of sin new to you? How does it help you understand Paul's way of thinking and his address to the congregation? Do you think the well-being of creation and of each creature (including us) is utterly dependent on the Creator? Explain.

• Read Romans 1:19-20. Paul asserts that what is known and knowable about God is readily and easily seen. Do you agree? Explain. How do you know what you think you know about God?

• Romans 1:18-32 is often cited in arguments against same-sex orientation and relationships. Some scholars claim this is a direct prohibition of homosexuality; others see in it a prohibition against cult prostitution or other worship practices that were degrading to the worshiper and to God. Given the corporate, rather than private or personal, condemnation of practices that injure the community, how does this passage inform you on the issue of right behavior? *Metaphore for general practices — God not human devotion*

[margin handwritten note: *Homosexuality passage*]

Divine Justice
Read Romans 2:1–3:20

In order to think objectively about Paul's argument as it unfolds in Romans 2, it may be helpful to consider his concept of salvation history and wonder to what extent

his theology may conflict with assumptions he makes on
the basis of his first-century Jewish background. Paul ①
conceived of God as both Judge and Savior. God's judgment would be accomplished at the close of history when
God would determine the fate of humanity on the basis of
their behavior (2:5-11). One of Paul's constant challenges
as he taught and functioned as a pastor was to defend the
integrity of God's justice and God's sovereignty. That is to
say, it was vital for Paul that God be understood as being
both consistently fair in rewarding and punishing and free
to save those whom God chose to spare from condemnation. At several points, Paul's readers might be led to
believe that God's grace will result in mercy "on the day of
wrath" for all those who have faith, without reference to
their deeds. Thus, the Protestant reformers emphasized
the doctrine of salvation by grace through faith alone. Yet
this passage clearly retains the earlier Jewish apocalyptic
concept of rewards and punishment on the basis of doing
"what the law requires" (2:14-16). This apparent contra-
diction functions in dialectic tension throughout this section of Romans, to be resolved later in Chapter 8.

A second concept, inherited this time from Greek philosophy, deserves consideration: conscience. Conscience ②
was understood as an innate faculty of all human beings
by which they could know both what is right and what is
wrong to do. Thus, Paul could conceive of a pagan nation
that nevertheless did what was acceptable to God and
that, therefore, would be excused by God at the Final
Judgment due to its ignorance of the Law and the
Prophets (Romans 2:14-16).

Chapter 2 provides the first clear evidence of Paul's use
of the diatribe, a teaching device familiar to Paul from his

background in rhetoric and Greek philosophy, which he employed to enhance the impact of his message.

The Diatribe   a bitter, often abrasive criticism or denunciation

The diatribe is a form of argumentation familiar in Paul's day, used, for example, by the Cynics and Stoics, as a means for raising philosophical questions that struck at the heart of humanity. This device placed questions on the lips of a hypothetical objector, or "straw man," so that the advocate, Paul, for example, could answer them.

The first-person plural "you" of Romans 2:1-5, and of verses 17-24 to a lesser degree, represents the straw man with whom Paul purports to argue his point. He is not assuming that all his readers are idolaters or that all his Jewish Christian readers in Rome break the Law, as it might appear (see 1:18; 2:8). Instead, Paul writes in the form of a diatribe to make a point about hypocrisy and the justice of God. God will judge us on the basis of our actions, not on the basis of our wisdom, ethnicity, or religious practices (2:13). Paul made this same point about the just consequences of rebellion against God in a more prosaic manner in 2:6-11. Paul's concern here emerged out of a controversy that had plagued his ministry from its inception.

In the early church, particularly outside of Jerusalem, two parties formed. One group had been converted to Christianity from paganism. They did not care to practice Jewish purity laws, to be circumcised, or to observe the Jewish sabbath. That is to say, they had no desire to become Jews in order to be considered full participants in the kingdom of God. The other party is known today as the "Judaizers." They believed that Gentile converts to Christianity needed to be circumcised and to attend to all other aspects of Jewish life. If they failed to do so, the Judaizers considered the Gentile converts inferior and ostracized them at fellowship meals (Galatians 2:11-14). Paul sought to resolve this controversy by asserting, "For a person is not a Jew who is one outwardly. . . . Real circumcision is a matter of the heart—it is spiritual and not literal" (Romans 2:28-29).   *another metaphor*

The motivation behind this controversy may well have been more than political infighting or ethnic rivalry. The Jewish Christians who continued to practice the complex and demanding requirements of Judaism may have sensed some inequity within the Christian community. Was it fair or right that God would require all this of them and not of God's Gentile offspring? What was the value of bothering to be Jewish if the majority of Christians were excused from carrying that weight of responsibility?

Paul addressed this point of view in Chapter 3, using the diatribe in verses 1-8. Again, he set up an argument with an imaginary debater. Paul found deep meaning and great honor, personally, in being Jewish; for to his people were "entrusted . . . the oracles of God," that is, the Hebrew Scriptures, the covenant promises, and the prophetic writings (Romans 3:2). Paul believed that the Law remained God's standard of judgment for all people, though it belongs to the Jews (3:19). On the other hand, the Law serves chiefly to warn people of their transgressions against what can otherwise be known through nature itself; "for through the law comes the knowledge of sin" (3:20; see also 2:15-16). In the end, Paul wanted to impose circumcision and purity laws on no one. Instead, he wanted to inspire respect both for the religious heritage of the Jews and for the religious freedom of the Gentile Christians.

The mid-section of Chapter 3 is highly significant to Paul's argument and somewhat difficult to reconcile with the audience he originally addressed. On the one hand, he calls for mutual respect and openness, addressing his readers as faithful and beloved of God. On the other hand, he asserts that all are under the power of sin (3:9-18).

Current scholars, most notably Luke Timothy Johnson, believe that this passage is also best understood as diatribe.[2] That is to say, Paul used this form of debate to make a fundamental point about humanity's need for salvation and about the inability of the law (or any particular set of religious practices) to save anyone. He used the rhetoric of opposites to demonstrate his point in bold relief. Paul is about to declare, "All have sinned and fall short of the glory of God" (3:23). All people, Jews and Greeks, need the salvation made available to them through Jesus Christ.

In summary, Paul argued that all people have sinned against God and deserve God's wrath. All deserve to be condemned and, through self-destructive practices, condemn themselves. No particular religious or ethnic group has any advantage over anyone else. All come under the judgment of God. All are guilty, each in his or her particular way. The Hebrew Torah, particularly the Decalogue (or Ten Commandments of Exodus 20:1-17; 34:28), only serves to make the Jews aware of their guilt. Nevertheless, in knowing the law, they also have the advantage of knowing the nature of God's will and the justice of God's judgment.

DIVINE JUSTICE

• Read Romans 2:1-16. How does this passage explain God's justice and how that justice is meted out? What does Paul mean by "law," and how is that law applied? What does law have to do with behavior and with justice?

• Consider Romans 2:17-29. What is the argument of the Judaizers concerning circumcision? What is Paul's response about the inward and outward signs of keeping God's covenant?

• Note that Paul encouraged the Romans to practice what they preached (2:17-24). What are the most challenging demands of the faith for you to keep? How do you deal with your own inconsistent behavior? What does your own struggle teach you about judging others?

• Read Romans 3:1-20. Recall a circumstance in which you felt that the demands placed on you were more onerous than those placed on someone else. What was your reaction? Can you identify with the Judaizers? Why or why not?

• In Romans 3:9-18, Paul quotes and combines several of the Hebrew Scriptures to demonstrate that all sin and that no one is truly righteous. Do you agree with that? If this is so, what hope do we have? If all are in need of salvation, how is that accomplished? Is salvation possible for those who refuse to believe? for those who "worship the creature rather than the Creator"? for those who refuse to follow the established worship practices of their religious community? for those who engage in the list of vices of Romans 1:29-32? Explain.

IN CLOSING

• Summarize the Scriptures and text for this session. What are the most compelling points or newest ideas? In what Scriptures do you find the most hope? the most challenge? the greatest threat? the best opportunity for spiritual growth?

• Join together in prayer for all those who are in need of the salvation of Jesus Christ. Pray as well for the insight to be able to see wherein you have sinned and fall short and for the grace and strength to overcome your shortcomings.

---

[1] From "The Practices of Romans 1:26: Homosexual or Heterosexual," by James E. Miller, in *Novum Testamentum* (Volume 37, 1995); pages 1–11.

[2] From *Reading Romans*, by Luke Timothy Johnson (The Crossroad Publishing Company, 1997); page 43.

III THE GOSPEL OF OUR LORD JESUS CHRIST

God's Righteousness Revealed
Read Romans 3:21-26

Having established the universal human need to be set free from enslavement to sin, Paul announced the great good news: Freedom has been gained for all through the faithfulness of God in Jesus' death and resurrection (Romans 3:21-26). This fuller presentation of the gospel, first described in the thesis statement, clearly names the role Jesus played in bringing about the salvation Paul announced. Still, the emphasis is on God and God's action on behalf of humankind. In this passage Paul insists on God's goodness and fairness but moves beyond them to God's mercy and great gift in Jesus Christ.

Several key terms and phrases used within this fuller proclamation merit attention. First, verse 21 uses the term *disclosed* to indicate what happened in Jesus' death and resurrection. The significance of this terminology may be to suggest that now something is known that previously had not been fully known, as opposed to making known something that had not been known at all. The distinction is significant at several levels, one of which influences the way Paul's theory of atonement is interpreted (Romans 3:25a).

Was Jesus' death a requisite sacrifice to satisfy God's

justice, as if God needed to be paid off, or a sign to all of God's mercy, forever characteristic of God's nature as "attested by the law and the prophets" (Romans 3:21)? Any careful reading of the Torah, the Prophets, and the Psalms will reveal frequent affirmations of the ongoing mercy of God in the Hebrew tradition. The death and resurrection of Jesus do not prove something that had not previously been true of God. They simply manifest that truth boldly and thus make it more available. God is good and always has been, in Paul's mind.

The second key phrase appears in verse 22, which standard translations (KJV, RSV, and NRSV) interpret as "through faith in Jesus Christ." This is an inaccurate translation of the Greek phrase, according to Luke Timothy Johnson and other scholars, as indicated by the footnote in the NRSV. The phrase should be translated directly from the Greek, respecting the grammar of the original, as "through the faith of Jesus Christ." Further support for this correction comes from within the NRSV itself when the same Greek phrase is later translated "through the righteousness of faith" (4:13). The significance of this correction has implications for the further development of Paul's thesis in Chapter 9, when Paul deals with the salvation of the Jews by faith. This correction also has significant implications for world missions, as well as for monotheism and Christianity's standing in the interfaith community.

Consider the exclusivism that would be implied by Paul in suggesting that the one God of all people would require everyone to believe in someone or something they may not know of or understand in order to win God's mercy (see Romans 10:14-15). We need to be aware of Paul's teaching in Romans 2:14-16 concerning Gentiles without the

[margin handwritten note: from Christ to us — not via versa]

law who nevertheless do what God requires. The issue there is not obeying the religious law or ascribing to a particular creed but doing what is right, as Jesus did what is right, toward God and humankind. Consider also Paul's treatise on the salvation of the Jews in which he does not mention their having to confess faith in Jesus in order to be saved (Romans 11:26-32). Their salvation is simply God's act for the benefit of God's people. Conversely, in contrast to previous references, note Paul's seemingly exclusivist statement in Romans 10:9-13. Paul himself may, however, have moved between two positions on this matter, unsettled as he was about the inclusion of his fellow Jews in God's salvation.

"The faith of Jesus," or Jesus' faith, was none other than perfect obedience to the will of God. Jesus, the righteous one, was willingly put to death under the law. But in the death and resurrection of Jesus Christ, God established a new righteousness, which we see revealed in Jesus' act. The substance of the faith that Paul's gospel required of humankind was not recognition of Jesus' death as an atoning sacrifice for the sins of the world but as obedience to God. One does not nullify the other, however. The issue is similar to the debate over whether Gentile Christians need to keep the Jewish purity laws and be circumcised in order to be children of God. God is one and the same for all people and requires the same of all consistently. The problem is not an individual's creed but humankind's inability to honor God in attitude and behavior. This is the significance of Paul's famous words, "All have sinned and fall short of the glory of God" (Romans 3:23). (Please note that the same phrase erroneously translated "faith in Jesus" reappears in verse 26 and should be read there, as in verse 21, "the faith of Jesus.")

The second term *justification* derives from the legal system of Paul's day. He used the term as a way of alluding to the Final Judgment and to God's justice. Inasmuch as Paul was eager to preserve respect for the justice of God and for God's merciful nature—both within the domain of God's sovereignty—Paul saw in God the right to acquit or justify the sinner regardless of his or her merit. No one deserved to be called innocent. No one deserved God's mercy. And yet all who believed the gospel were accounted righteous by God because of their faith. Nevertheless, the intent and power of the gospel was not only to acquit but also to bring about real righteousness: a right relationship with God based in faithful obedience and gracious relationships with others.

The third term is *justified* and should be interpreted in light of the controversy over purity laws. The point here is that no amount of obedience to any set of rules can create a righteous human being. To be justified is not merely a forensic reality, an imputed state, as many have taught. From Paul's perspective, to be justified is a matter of having a right relationship with God through practical obedience. Only a faithful acceptance of God's grace can make a person pure before God.

The fourth term that deserves careful attention is *gift* or *grace*, alternative translations of the same Greek word. Paul's theological priority is clearly on God's grace, not with humankind's faith. This emphasis retained its power for Paul because of the defining event of his spiritual journey: his conversion and call. Above all, that revelation was for him an experience of a great "gift": undeserved reconciliation with God leading to full submission to God's authority. Paul perceived even his own faith response to the revelation as being more a gift than a matter of his own choice. By grace Paul had come to know, in the most intimate sense, something he had not previously known.

Paul presents the gospel as "gift" in a variety of passages. Paul commended the Corinthian congregation who, by their good hearts and graceful conduct, were their own best "letter" attesting to the gift of the Spirit (2 Corinthians 3:1-4). Likewise with the Romans, Paul recognized that it was by the power of the Spirit, not by their own will, that the believers made their confession of faith: "When we cry, 'Abba! Father!' it is that very Spirit bearing witness with our spirit that we are children of God" (Romans 8:15-16). The Christian experience was, above all, God's goodness at work.

A fifth key term is *redemption*. Its significance to Christian vocabulary is enormous. The term refers to a ransom for the release of a prisoner that was, in its earliest usage, achieved by a payment to the captor by a kinsman. It functions as metaphor for the liberation of humankind from God's just condemnation.

The related term *atonement* clearly derives from the Torah and Jewish sacrificial practices, as well as from the prophetic tradition (Romans 3:25a; compare Mark 10:45; 14:24). The sacrifice of animals, birds, grains, and incense formed a core of the Hebrew worship and was a means to reconciliation with God. Human sacrifice was known in Palestine and was occasionally practiced (see, for example, 2 Kings 3:26-27; 16:2-3; 21:1-6), but it was considered abhorrent to the Hebrews and to God. The metaphor, therefore, should not be taken literally. Instead, it should be understood as a reference to communion with God, poetically described in terms of standing before God's mercy seat. Refer to the notation in the NRSV offering the alternative translation for Romans 3:24-25a, "the redemption that is in Christ Jesus, whom God put forward as a place of atonement." For believers, the empty cross of Jesus is the mercy seat of God, the symbolic "place" of our "atonement" with God.

In sum, Paul's gospel proclaims the righteousness of God as most clearly revealed in Jesus' death and resurrection. God has given humankind the gift of assurance of reconciliation with God, much as God gave the Hebrews a means of assurance of reconciliation through their sacrificial system, particularly the blood sacrifice of atonement (Leviticus 17:11). True reconciliation becomes effective through "the obedience of faith." This faith is itself a gift.

GOD'S RIGHTEOUSNESS REVEALED

• Read Romans 3:21-26 and identify the six key terms. What do those terms mean? How does Paul use them to make his point about God's justifying righteousness?
• How would you describe what happens to the believer who is justified? redeemed? What does it mean to you that Jesus Christ is "a place of atonement" for you personally, as well as for all humankind?
• What does this passage tell you about the nature of God?

Salvation by Faith
Read Romans 3:27–4:25

In this section Paul sets up both a debate with a generic Jewish boaster and a rhetorical opposition (Romans 3:27-31). (He later resolves the opposition by way of illustration and midrash on the Abrahamic tradition in Chapter 4.) For teaching purposes he set works of the Law over against faith. Paul's point is that no one can earn freedom from the taint of sin by his or her own effort. It is God who justifies. No one can be considered pure before God except on the basis of faith.

Midrash   Exegesis

Midrash is a method of Scripture interpretation that has been used for centuries by rabbis to exegete (understand and analyze) the text to find in it its inner significance, the principles or laws for living, and what it reveals about authentic religion.

Again Paul emphasizes the universality and sovereignty of God (3:29-30). Paul implies that if his readers (or his debate partner) are truly monotheists rather than pagans who worship the god of their particular nation or religious group, they will have to admit to the validity of his assertion: "Or is God the God of Jews only? Is he not the God of Gentiles also? Yes, of Gentiles also, since God is one; and he will justify the circumcised on the ground of faith and the uncircumcised through that same faith" (3:29-30).

Paul continues the rhetorical device of the diatribe in verse 31. Paul writes as if he is responding to an imaginary debater who accuses him, as many real opponents had, of overthrowing the Jewish law. Paul declares that his gospel upholds the law in a fuller sense than does the best of Jewish practice.

Notice how Paul attributed Abraham's right relationship with God to the fact that "Abraham believed God" (4:3). Since Paul always oriented himself in light of his original conversion and call and the revelation he received, he identified with Abraham personally. Paul considered Abraham to have come to know a profound truth, which he could not have known otherwise, by way of revelation. "After these things the word of the LORD came to Abram in a vision, 'Do not be afraid, Abram, I am your shield: your reward shall be very great.' But Abram said, 'O LORD GOD, what will you give me, for I continue childless, and the heir of my house is Eliezer of Damascus?'

And Abram said, 'You have given me no offspring, and so a slave born in my house is to be my heir.' But the word of the LORD came to him, 'This man shall not be your heir; no one but your very own issue shall be your heir.' He brought him outside and said, 'Look toward heaven and count the stars, if you are able to count them.' Then he said to him, 'So shall your descendants be.' And he believed the LORD; and the LORD reckoned it to him as righteousness" (Genesis 15:1-6). The truth about God was "disclosed" to Abraham, much as it was to Paul and as it is now to those who hear his gospel. Here again Paul emphasizes faith as "gift," since it comes by way of revelation (Romans 4:4).

Paul took considerable liberty in applying the Genesis material to his debate about God's revelation in Jesus Christ. The rabbis' vocation included reinterpreting the Law in order to make it relevant to the contemporary needs of God's people. By making reference to Genesis 12:3 to interpret Genesis 17:5 and then using both passages to buttress his argument about righteousness in Romans 4, Paul followed the honored rabbinic practice of midrash. In order to examine this midrashic work, refer to his including Gentile Christians, by implication, among the descendants of Abraham (Romans 4:16-18). Here Paul extended the meaning of Genesis 17:5 beyond the blood descendants of Abraham to include all those who respond to God with faith. Also note Paul's midrashic interpretation of the birth of Isaac to Sarah and Abraham in their old age as a virtual resurrection from the dead (Romans 4:19-25).

Paul used creative ingenuity to find precedent for the resurrection of Jesus from the dead in Sarah's conception of Isaac. Note also Paul's delight in Abraham's trust in

God's promise to give him a legitimate heir: Abraham was "fully convinced" (Romans 4:21). It was this trust in God's promise that Paul took as the model for faith rather than the seal of the promise, that is, circumcision. According to Paul, the righteous are those who trust God's promise of mercy disclosed in Jesus' death and resurrection, apart from "works of the law" (4:23-25).

SALVATION BY FAITH

• How would you compare Abraham's experiences with Paul's conversion and call?

• What is midrash, and how does Paul use it to explain his concept of righteousness? How do you use Scripture and learnings from your previous education and experience to interpret and analyze events, new ideas, and present experiences?

• Do you experience faith as a gift? as an effort? as both or neither? How does your faith become something you know, believe, and do all at the same time? In what practical and spiritual ways do you see yourself living out your faith?

The New Life of Obedience and Righteousness
Read Romans 5:1-17

Having established the means of salvation as being a gift of God to be received by faith, Paul proceeded to focus on the results of this saving faith. In so doing, he established a point of reference in the distant past in the person of Adam. Adam was credited as being the first human to rebel against God and to suffer the consequences. Paul conceived of Adam as being a son of God, "a type of the one who was to come" (Romans 5:14), that is, Jesus. The figure Adam represented the first Creation. Paul thus established a point of reference in the future: the

divine judgment and "eternal life" (5:21). These references, past and future, in turn established a context for
valuing the present: the work of Jesus Christ (the first-
born of the new creation) and the righteousness that char-
acterizes believers (see Romans 6:19-22). Paul's point is
that salvation is from something toward something; and,
moreover, that on the way there, salvation brings godli-
ness. Being in a right relationship with God is not merely
a Christian longing or hope. It is a current reality (5:1-2).
The agency of this new and right relationship with God is
the Holy Spirit.

Paul's conception of the Holy Spirit comes from his own
personal experience and that of his converts. The same
Spirit that was in Jesus now lives in the church. To
receive this gift of God's presence is to receive a love that
gives itself away for the well-being of others (5:5). To
receive the Spirit is to become a part of God's new creation, for the same breath of life by which Adam was
created is the Spirit by which believers are made truly
new (see Genesis 2:7; 2 Corinthians 5:17).

Again the reader will hear an echo of Paul's personal
experience of conversion and call. Paul wrote, "But God
proves his love for us in that while we still were sinners
Christ died for us" (Romans 5:8). Paul remained in awe of
the fact that the risen Christ would care enough about
him, an individual sinner, to appear to him and save him.
Thus the second-person plural in verse 8 is not simply a
reference to abstract humanity but a reference to personal
love giving itself for each person (see Galatians 2:20).

In comparing and contrasting Adam and Jesus, Paul
developed the ground of his claim of eternal life for all
who by faith obey God. Adam died, not because he was
mortal, but because he sinned. Death was the conse-

quence of humankind's transgression against God. Inasmuch as Jesus obeyed God even in death, Jesus, in resurrection, overcame the curse of death. Jesus' death and resurrection have given all humankind full access to the throne room of God; assurance of salvation; and a return to God's original intention for humanity, that is, eternal life. By eternal life, Paul refers to sharing in the quality of life revealed in the risen Christ. In seeking to interpret eternal life, Paul surely must have called upon not only his early Pharisaic belief in the bodily resurrection at the close of history but also his own visionary experience of the glorious Christ.

THE NEW LIFE OF OBEDIENCE AND RIGHTEOUSNESS

• Read Romans 5:1-17. How does Paul describe Adam? What does it mean for Adam to be a "type of the one to come"? How would you describe Paul's comments on Adam's death through his sin and trespass and the role Jesus Christ plays as the "new Adam" in justifying and redeeming that sinfulness? What does that mean for humankind?

Answering Objections
Read Romans 5:18–7:25

Romans 5:18-21, if read out of context, sounds like a proclamation of universal salvation or an act of God requiring no particular response from humankind. When Romans 5:18-21 is set in the context of the entire letter, however, the objective reader will recognize that Paul is using a rhetorical flourish or an overstatement of the case in order to underscore the contrast between life with and without the revelation in Jesus Christ. Paul is not saying that due to Jesus' righteousness everyone is automatically considered righteous. Paul is saying, rather, that those who respond to the revelation in Jesus with faith overcome their enslavement to sin and gain the freedom to live a life pleasing to God.

After having delineated the key points of his argument, Paul pauses to address some secondary concerns that he believes could legitimately emerge from his opposition. First, he faced the argument of the enthusiast who might want to take Paul's focus on the free gift of God in Jesus Christ to its logical conclusion by saying, "Well, if God is so interested in gifting us and the more sinful we are the greater God's gift, then let's get really rowdy!" (see Romans 6:1). Second, he addresses the small minority of believers who thought they could live an undisciplined life and escape the consequences. Inadvertently, this section also addresses the teaching of later scholars and preachers who taught that believers are both justified before God and sinners, as if God no longer required righteousness. Paul responds to these opponents with the affirmation, "Therefore we have been buried with him by baptism into death, so that, just as Christ was raised from the dead by the glory of the Father, so we too might walk in newness of life" (6:4).

Paul used what must have been an earlier understanding of the sacrament of baptism to establish the radical nature of the new life (6:3-7). The practice of baptism in the early church was often, but not only, by immersion in running water. The concept was that the person who was submerged in the waters of baptism died to his or her old self under the power of this symbolic bath. The pollution of the old life was washed away. As the convert emerged from the water, it was as if God raised him or her from the dead, spritually and morally new, to share the resurrection life of the glorified Christ. As Jesus died and rose again, forever freed from the curse of mortality, so also the believers must consider themselves "dead to sin and alive to God" (Romans 6:11).

The diatribe and exhortation that follow in verses 12-19 draw on the metaphor of slavery and the assumption that everyone serves someone or something. In the old life, the believer served the passions of the flesh, resulting in sin and death. (For Paul, "flesh" refers to physicality as well as to the human's penchant for sin or weakness.) In the new life, the believer serves God, resulting in righteousness and "sanctification" (6:14, 19). The believers at Rome, called to be saints, have been set apart for the service of God and have been made holy as God is holy. Note that Paul stepped out of the diatribe to return to a thanksgiving for the Christians at Rome in verses 17-18, declaring their righteousness and faith to be obedience "from the heart." It was this inner response of faith and joyful submission to the authority of God, leading to doing what God wills, that Paul understood to be the goal of his gospel (1:5). Clearly this gospel was not for the careless enthusiast who wanted to avoid moral and spiritual accountability.

In the final section of this set of responses to objectors, Paul introduces the problem of shame (6:21). Previously, when speaking in forensic terms, Paul spoke from the perspective of the sinner's guilt. Before God the Judge, the sinner is guilty. Before God the merciful and Holy One, the sinner is ashamed. In contrast, the believer is not only acquitted before the Judge but also sanctified to a life of holiness, ultimately to gain eternal communion with God.

In Chapter 7, Paul set up further oppositions: flesh versus spirit and "the old written code" versus "the new life of the Spirit" (7:6). His first illustration, regarding marriage and remarriage, has failed to communicate over the centuries because many people become so entangled within the illustration that they miss the point (7:1-6). Paul was simply saying that Christians are to live toward the law as if the law were dead. Metaphorically, they are free to remarry. They can unite themselves with the new order (salvation by the faith of Jesus) so as to enter an entirely new life. It is to be as if they had previously been married to sin and are now married to God. The purpose of this illustration parallels the earlier use of the metaphor of slavery.

Paul's second illustration is presented as another diatribe: "Well, then, you have relegated the law to the category of sin!" (see Romans 7:7). Paul's response is to deny the charge and to insist that while the law is holy and good, its function is to make the transgressor aware that he or she has sinned against God. Paul also suggests that awareness of what God forbids functions as a lure for the guilty to become even more guilty. The law cannot correct the moral and spiritual failure of transgressors; it only makes them aware of their helpless condition. The law can redeem no one. It is powerless to bring about positive change.

Romans 7:14-25 addresses the next logical objection that Paul's opponents might well have raised out of a pricked conscience. They may have said, "Very well. But the fact is that I still do things that I know to be wrong, even though I don't want to. I can't seem to help myself!" In order to respond most effectively to this far less rhetorical objection, Paul used a first-person narrative. He impersonated the objector and described in moving detail the inner conflict being posed. In so doing, he slipped into an "either/or" opposition between flesh and spirit that must not be generalized as a total repudiation of the value of the human body (Romans 7:18 and 25b). As a corrective, note the several references to the body as the dwelling place of God in the Spirit within Paul's other letters (see 1 Corinthians 6:19; 2 Corinthians 4:10; Philippians 1:20). This first-person narrative is a mask behind which the debater speaks in order to portray the human condition apart from the redemptive power of the gospel. Romans 7:14-25 is not autobiographical. The debater concludes his argument with an act of thanksgiving, an affirmation of faith, claiming that through Jesus Christ he is released from the bondage of sin (7:25).

ANSWERING OBJECTIONS

• Read Romans 5:18–6:23. What does it mean for grace to abound where sin had multiplied? Does that give us license to sin more boldly?
• Does God's grace excuse our sin without consequence? Explain. How did Paul use Jesus' death and resurrection as the key metaphor for the Christian experience? (See Romans 6:3-4.) What is the connection for Paul between baptism and resurrection imagery?
• Read Romans 7:1-25. What is the function of the law, according to Paul? (See Romans 7:5, 7-12.) What is the relationship of law and sin? How does Paul contrast flesh and spirit? the old, written code and the new life in the Spirit? In what ways do you see this contrast in daily life? What spiritual insight can you gain from these observations?
• Look more closely at Romans 7:14-25. How can the believer's physical life become a means of honoring God rather than being a cause for shame? How do you interpret and deal with your own inner conflicts between wrong and right desires?

IN CLOSING

• Summarize the key ideas in this text: revelation, the faith of Jesus, justified and justification, gift or grace, redemption, atonement, and others of interest to you. How do these foundations of our theology forge us into mature disciples?
• Join together in prayer for deep understanding of the saving grace of Jesus Christ; and if you feel led, make or renew your commitment as a disciple. Pray for those who struggle under the burden of sin without the knowledge of God's freedom.

IV THE SPIRITUAL LIFE OF THE CHRISTIAN

Paul's Spirituality

Like all of us, Paul was shaped emotionally and spiritually by marker events and influential relationships as well as by his religious training. The inner life of faith that informed the apostle's preaching and teaching as a pastor and founder of congregations had its roots in his formative experiences. According to Luke, Paul (Saul) was born in Tarsus (Acts 22:3). Tarsus was a university city of the Roman Empire and was quite diverse in its religious culture. It is clear that during Paul's years in this pagan city, he had ample opportunity to become acquainted with various mystery religions and cults that celebrated the dying and rising of their gods. This exposure was part of Paul's background as he moved from the Pharisaic belief in a general bodily resurrection of the dead on the final day of history to the Christian celebration of the individual resurrection of Jesus of Nazareth on the third day following his death. His knowledge of the tenets of various Greco-Roman philosophies and religions enabled Paul to use those concepts to help Gentile Christians and Gentile converts to understand that Jesus is the human and divine Son of God.

When Paul returned to Tarsus after spending some time in Arabia, he apparently associated with the philosophers of the universities in that cosmopolitan city. Their thinking influenced him. He developed a respect for the best of their insights and incorporated some elements of Greek philosophy into his own understanding of the structure, meaning, and purpose of life. This study may have sharpened his ability to employ tools of Greek rhetoric in the Epistle to the Romans, as well as to communicate the gospel in terms readily received by Westerners.

At the same time that Paul was influenced by the Greco-Roman culture of his home city, he was informed by his family's faith. Apparently Paul's father was a devout Jew, probably a Pharisee, who raised his son to understand himself in light of his spiritual identity as well as his ethnic identity (Philippians 3:5). He sent his son to Jerusalem for advanced religious education (Acts 22:3).

Paul's childhood education in the context of the synagogue and his later study at the feet of the famous rabbi, Gamaliel of Jerusalem, made him a devout Jew. He respected the Law, the Prophets, the sacred worship, and the sense of being chosen that belonged to all descendants of Abraham. Because of all this, Paul gave himself utterly to the study, practice, and defense of his religious heritage until his death. His zeal, however, may well have been balanced and challenged by the influence that his early teacher Gamaliel had on him well beyond his years as a student. It was most likely the same moderate Gamaliel who advised the Sanhedrin to restrain their power to execute the apostles because they may "even be found fighting against God!" (Acts 5:33-39).

The early Christian deacon Stephen and his community may also have provided a shaping influence on Paul's spirituality (Acts 7:54–8:1). Paul, in persecuting the fledgling colony of Christians, possibly saw and heard much that moved him to recognize a practice of faith and trust in God that transcended his own. Through Paul's exposure to Christians before his conversion, he was forced beyond his own religious boundaries and challenged by the faithfulness of people different from him.

The Pharisaic party of Judaism, of which Paul was an active member, was notoriously scrupulous regarding observance of the law. According to Martin Buber in his seminal study of Judaism and Christianity, *Two Types of Faith*, it was not, however, simply a religion focused on observing the purity laws, but one of trust based in historic experience of God.[1] This point is significant because many have assumed that Paul was burdened by a sense of guilt over having failed to keep the law adequately and was thus driven to proclaim a gospel of salvation by grace in a way that someone less burdened might not have. This estimate of Paul's spiritual struggle represents a relatively late, Western imposition upon the soul of Paul rather than a legitimate spiritual biography. Paul, by his own testimony, kept the law blamelessly (Philippians 3:4-6). As a Jew, he had been confident and even proud of his faithfulness to God.

Paul, the Pharisee, benefited from a remarkably enlightened monotheism, as illustrated by the theological assumptions he made in writing to the church at Rome. He trusted the God revealed in Torah to be inscrutable (Romans 11:33). Paul accepted the worldview of his forefathers to be a matter of divine revelation making plain for all to see that the one true and living God was fair, good, and trustworthy, always working on the stage of history for the salvation of creation. Paul's Jewish faith taught him to expect God to make God's self known by way of special revelation, while remaining invisible. Thus, when Paul had his dramatic conversion experience on the road to Damascus, it was an epiphany—a manifestation of God—that he readily accepted. Paul remained an active, practicing Jew at least through the time of his arrest in Jerusalem, just after he wrote the Letter to the Romans, in spite of the accusations against him to the contrary (see Acts 21:27-29).

On the other hand, even though Paul's Jewish credentials were a matter of pride and strength for him, he could call it all "rubbish" (Philippians 3:7-9). This attitude on Paul's part toward his past has incensed Jews like Martin Buber, inasmuch as Paul implied that he found something superior to the Jewish faith and traded that for his rich heritage. Even worse, Paul has frequently been charged with inciting anti-Semitism in the church by way of his writing. A careful study of Paul's spirituality and theology will prove, however, that, far from being anti-Semitic, Paul loved his people enough to be willing to die for them, both physically and spiritually (Romans 9:1-5).

When he spoke of the comparison between his inherited faith and his Christian faith, Paul declared that he found in his relationship with Christ something far greater than his own accomplishments as a zealous Pharisee. His many references to the Spirit suggest that he experienced the Holy Spirit as the Spirit of Christ alive and present within the church. This direct experience of the Spirit created the possibility for a personal relationship with Christ. That relationship with Christ was for him born of a divine disclosure, sustained by the indwelling Holy Spirit, and manifest in a passionate love for his Jewish kin as well as for the Gentile world.

Jewish Scripture and prayer forms, as well as sabbath keeping, remained sacred elements of Paul's lifestyle until his death; but Paul developed a dynamic and spontaneous prayer life as well. Apparently Paul's personal practice of prayer extended beyond the traditional prayers used in public worship on the sabbath. He wrote that he prayed in the Spirit and spoke in tongues more than any of the charismatics at Corinth (1 Corinthians 14:18). Paul enjoyed a deep sense of communion with God through the Spirit's intercession (Romans 8:26). On several occasions, the Spirit provided him with guidance and discernment for the direction of his ministry, as well as deep inner assurance (2 Corinthians 12:1-7). Paul also actively prayed for his fellow Jews and for believers in every community he had organized. Moreover, he relied on his fellow believers to pray fervently for the effectiveness of his mission (for example, Romans 15:30-33).

Wherever Paul went, he found Jews and Jewish sympathizers whose love for God made them receptive to his message. Their knowledge of and respect for Scripture compelled them to accept Jesus as the fulfillment of God's Word. On the other hand, the majority of Jews with whom Paul argued in the synagogues of the Roman Empire rejected his message and, in many cases, mistreated him. No doubt Paul developed a sense of alienation and personal pain relative to his fellow Jews, a divided loyalty he struggled with in his letter to the church at Rome (Romans 9–11). This alienation caused him at times to characterize Jewish tradition as a religion of the law, the opposite of life in the Spirit (Romans 8; Galatians 3:1-2, 10-14).

Because it was Paul's zeal for the law that drove him to persecute the early church, he may have harbored a certain antipathy for his Jewish heritage. Paul may well have felt that his religion had betrayed him by blinding him to the truth that the very people he persecuted had openly received. He likely felt that he was guilty of fighting against God because of the religion he defended so tenaciously. Thus, Paul may have felt that the law had wounded him. If so, he, like the disabled Jewish beggar whom Peter and John healed in Jesus' name (Acts 3:1-10), found himself leaping and walking and praising God once he discovered the faith of Jesus. The zeal and love he had invested in defending his inherited faith, he transferred to the work of proclaiming Jesus as the fulfillment of all Israel's highest hopes (Galatians 1:13-17). The once wounded Paul had become a healed soul, freed to endure with great tenacity a broad set of challenges to his invincible faith (2 Corinthians 11:23-33).

Although Paul's formative experiences in some ways defined his spiritual domain, he was directed by the Spirit away from conservatism to lead the people of God into a new future. As a result of his conversion and call, he shifted his energies from preserving his heritage to spreading the kingdom of God. Paul's vision was always informed by his revelatory experience of the glorious Christ, and his hope was always set on sharing that glory with Christ and with all those who were called to be saints in this life and throughout eternity.

PAUL'S SPIRITUALITY

• What do you recall of Paul's early life? What shaped his beliefs? How did the intermingling of Greco-Roman and Jewish philosophy and religion shape Paul's spirituality? What intercultural experiences have you had that helped forge your identity? your faith? your understanding of others? your ways of interpreting events and worldview?

• Read the Scriptures in this section from Philippians 3. What more do you learn about Paul's background? What were the primary influences in your own personal and spiritual development?

• Note the spiritual disciplines Paul observed (keeping the law and the sabbath, prayer, discernment, reliance on his tradition for guidance to the future). How did these disciplines serve him? What disciplines do you employ for your own growth? How do they serve you? help you serve God and neighbor?

Life in the Spirit
Read Romans 8:1-17

In Romans 8, Paul finally arrived at the climax of his gospel. He celebrated the result of the saving work of God in Jesus' death and resurrection by the agency of the Holy Spirit. He proclaimed the good news that "the just requirement of the law" may now be fulfilled in those who "walk not according to the flesh, but according to the Spirit" (8:4). Paul believed that by the power of the Spirit, believers can overcome the universal human proclivity toward sin and gain a righteous and eternal quality of life like unto that of Christ.

In order to appreciate the underlying logic of this significant section of Paul's argument, it may help to explore the paradigm that informed Paul's thought: Jesus died in the flesh and rose in the Spirit. For Paul, Jesus' death and resurrection formed the pivotal point in the fulcrum of salvation history. Moreover, for Paul that bodily transformation of Jesus parallels, in a vivid and profoundly symbolic way, the transformation that occurs when people receive the gift of faith. The change that takes place in the believer by the agency of the Spirit moves him or her from a mere temporal mind/body existence into life in the Spirit and anticipates his or her eternal life in the presence of God. While this paradigm serves as the foundation of Paul's logic, a specific theory of salvation derived from this paradigm of death and resurrection shapes his message.

Paul's doctrine of salvation, including the universality of sin, justification by grace through faith, and sanctification by the Word and Holy Spirit (all of which he presented in Romans 1–7), emerged directly from Paul's understanding of Jesus' death and resurrection. As Paul understood him, Jesus lived and died without ever having sinned (5:18-19; 8:2-3). Unlike anyone before him, Jesus lived and died in full submission to the will of God, never having turned aside toward any competing influence. Therefore, his life and death could be likened to the unblemished sacrifice of a perfect lamb offered as a sacrifice of atonement for sin (8:3).

Moreover, Jesus was a man who lived and died under the guidance and inspiration of the Spirit. His death, therefore, did not lead to bodily corruption, as death had for every other human being from the time of Adam's expulsion from the garden of Eden. Instead, Jesus rose from the dead and was given a glorious, immortal body by which the horror of sin and death was exposed in bold relief and then overcome. Having been raised from the dead by the transforming power of the Holy Spirit, the risen Christ gave his Spirit to the church (8:9a). Thus, as believers die to their past devotions and turn from their false gods to serve the living God revealed in Jesus Christ, they are likewise set free by the Holy Spirit from the tomb of their moral and spiritual corruption to lead a truly new life in which they belong to God (8:9b). It is for them as if they too have been raised from the dead (8:11). They have the guarantee, sealed by the ever-present Spirit, that they belong to God and will share the resurrection life of Christ beyond physical death. With this background in plain view, Romans 8 becomes translucent. The condemnation from which the believer is set free is clearly that of moral corruption in life and bodily corruption in death.

Paul used several terms that, when understood as he intended them, serve to illumine his meaning and make the gospel accessible. A set of terms revolves around Paul's dualism of flesh versus Spirit (*sarx* and *soma* in Greek). The term *flesh* refers to the physical and appetitive nature of the human being, the bodily dimension of human life that is mortal and neutral, but which invariably leads all through their weakness to sin and "fall short of the glory of God." Paul did not despise the physical but called for its sanctification. Sanctification refers to the cleansing and consecrating of the entire human self—body, mind, and spirit—to the service of God. The spirit of the human being, the heart, can commune with the Holy Spirit, which dwells within the believer (8:27). Paul made a definite distinction between the spirit or heart of the human being that seeks after God and the Spirit of Christ or of God that is "poured into our hearts" (5:5).

Now the dualism between flesh and spirit and between law and faith that surfaced in Romans 3 and 4 resurfaces here in Paul's argument, this time with a greater sense of triumph. Paul reasserts that the law cannot save humanity from its tendency to live according to its own self-destructive, God-denying agenda, that is, according to the flesh (8:3a). Only God can do so, and God has indeed rescued humankind. The liberation that Paul describes as life in the Spirit is a turning of the soul; a radical change of mind; a total reorientation toward a life that is inspired, informed, and empowered by the divine Spirit (8:14).

With this new life comes a deep assurance of one's security in relationship with God as the Holy Spirit within the

believers inspires their worship (8:16). This assurance of
salvation expressed in a Spirit-inspired affirmation of faith,
"Abba! Father!" (8:15b), functions as a foretaste of eternal communion with God and God's family. It is a glorious
glimpse into all that can be anticipated beyond the present
suffering of persecution and the constant threat of
martyrdom (8:17). The dialectic has been resolved. The
potentially sinful "flesh" is transformed to the dwelling
place of God in the Spirit, now and for eternity. The judging function of the law becomes the positive law of life in
the Spirit, God-given and now being fulfilled (Romans 8:4).

The Christian experience did not assume that the Spirit
of God or of Christ dwelt in all flesh from birth, though it
credited God as being the source of life. Instead, the
church experienced an outpouring of the Spirit that
occurred when the seeker after God came to believe the
gospel and to submit with obedience to the will of God.
Paul taught, in full harmony with the Hebrew Scriptures,
that God is holy and that God's Holy Spirit cannot dwell
in an unclean temple. Since all have sinned and cannot
escape the moral and spiritual pollution of their transgressions, a radical cleansing and redemption are prerequisite
to the experience of communion with God in the Spirit.

LIFE IN THE SPIRIT

• Read Romans 8:3-11. How did Paul differentiate between "flesh" and
the believer's bodily existence? Paul uses the term *flesh* in more than
one way—as physicality and as a penchant for sin and weakness. In
Jewish belief, "flesh" was morally neutral but could be corrupted to sin.
How do you understand the distinction between flesh and spirit? In
your experience, is life in the spirit totally opposed to and distinct from
life in the flesh? If not, how do they overlap?

• Read Romans 8:12-17. What does it mean to live in the flesh or to live in the Spirit? to be heirs of God and joint heirs with Christ? Do you see yourself as an heir? What does this mean to your life and faith? What does it mean to have to suffer because of this inheritance? Can you "give back" this inheritance to avoid the suffering? If so, would you want to? Explain.

Salvation for All Creation Through Crisis
Read Romans 8:18-39

Paul suffered for his faith and knew that his fellow believers in Rome had likewise been forced to endure hardships and prejudice as a direct result of their religious identity. In line with the great suffering servant psalms of Deutero-Isaiah (Isaiah 40–55), most notably Isaiah 53, Paul believed that the suffering of believers was a significant part of the redemptive work of God for the sake of creation. God was using the anguish of God's people to bring about the salvation of the world. Nevertheless, in the midst of the suffering, God's people must look beyond the difficulty to the triumph that lies ahead in order to remain patient and to find courage.

In this remarkable passage, Paul expands his focus on God's saving work beyond God's concern for humankind to include all of nature. But Paul was no environmentalist. He may even be accused of having, at times, a negative view of physical life. But here, in Romans 8:18-25, Paul moved into a profound empathy with creation, likening its suffering to the labor pains of a mother in childbirth. He perceived all of Creation to be in a divine crisis. A new era was being born, however (8:22). Out of this deep pain would come liberty and deliverance from tragedy, decay, and death. Although that release was not yet complete, it would come as surely as a baby will be delivered of a woman in travail. This is the whole world's vital and reliable hope, in spite of the appearance of things (8:24).

Paul refers in verse 26 to the weakness of fear, doubt, and confusion that can plague even the most devout when they find themselves threatened. That emotional and spiritual weakness will be met, Paul assured his readers, by the great power and grace of God's own presence, reaching out to raise the believer into a dynamic experience of the flow of divine energy. In the midst of anguish, the Spirit of Christ is present to assist the believer in prayer and to comfort the distressed. Paul used the term translated "sighs too deep for words" when describing the Spirit's intercession for the saints in their state of need (Romans 8:26b).

This profound personal experience of prayer, aided by a guidance and power beyond one's self, assures the believer of divine help in time of need and restores the believer's joy in communion with God. Paul understood the experience as being a matter of the Spirit's searching the depth of the believer, assessing his or her need, and mediating divine grace in a time of trouble and vulnerability. The believer hardly knows how to pray in the midst of crisis; so God's own Spirit prays effectively, according to God's saving purpose (Romans 8:27).

God's purpose is plain: that we shall be made like Christ (8:29). Both the believers' individual and corporate suffering, in consonance with Christ's suffering, death, and resurrection, will lead to the formation of a new humanity, a new family. This new creation will be counted innocent and will enjoy full and perfect communion with God, as does the risen Christ (8:30). God's original purpose in creating humankind in God's own image will be fulfilled.

Although John Calvin, and some of his followers today,

taught a doctrine of predestination and election based on Paul's use of the term *predestined* in verse 30, the term merely refers to God's intentional and effective work to accomplish the salvation of the world through Jesus Christ, as is made clear by the great affirmation that follows in verses 31-39. Paul's term *predestined* should not be read as implying an arbitrary act of God. To do so would exclude some from God's saving grace and admit others to eternal life regardless of their faith and actions, thereby robbing all of their assurance of salvation.

In the face of official interrogation and evil released without reserve, under the threat of martyrdom, throughout the false accusations and beatings, even while starving and dying, the believer can be sure that his or her communion with God remains uninterrupted and secure because God is always working for the salvation of the world (8:35-39). How can believers be defeated if the risen Christ, holding ultimate power over the course of history, prays for us (8:34)? In the end, Christ will conquer evil; and God's good purpose will triumph. Creation will emerge fresh; new; and nevermore to be plagued by violence, decay, and futility.

SALVATION FOR ALL CREATION THROUGH CRISIS

• Read Romans 8:18-25. What suffering is Paul talking about here? Describe how first-century Christians under Roman rule may have suffered for their faith and found it difficult to remain hopeful that God loved them and was indeed in charge.
• How would you describe the "groaning of creation" in this passage? in your own experience and environment? How will God's redemption change these "labor pains"?

• What does Paul mean by adoption and redemption of our bodies? How is this an image of hope? Where do you see hope for a world (or life) in travail?

• Read Romans 8:26-30. How have you experienced the Spirit of God praying through you? What is it like? How does it affect you when ithappens? Do you believe that all things work for good for those who love God? Does that mean that there should be no tragedy or difficulty? Explain.

• Read Romans 8:31-39. Do you know someone whose experience of tragedy has caused her or him to feel abandoned by God? How would Paul respond to such a person so as to inspire her or his faith? How can the average person be "more than a conquerer" over these huge, even cosmic, forces of life and death?

Apocalyptic Thought and Paul's Ministry to the Church at Rome

Apocalyptic thinking can emerge in any culture when its people despair of ever enjoying peace and well-being through human agency in this world. Apocalyptic thinking is usually characterized by visions filled with symbolic imagery of a catastrophic end of history. In this final conflict between good and evil, God defeats evil, vindicates the righteous, and punishes the unjust. Apocalyptic thought dominated the Jewish worldview in the first century and shaped Paul's expectation that the Christ would imminently return to bring God's saving purpose to consummation (Romans 8:18-25; 13:11-14; 16:20; 1 Thessalonians 5:2-3; 2 Thessalonians 1:5-12). Paul was himself experiencing great opposition and fighting discouragement at the time he wrote. He knew, moreover, that his fellow Jews in Rome had only recently returned from a long, forced exile under Roman persecution. These were troubled times for his new friends in Rome, as well as for him. Paul expected that all this suffering would lead to some great good and understood his mission to the church at Rome as an opportunity for mutual encouragement in a time of acute need (Romans 1:12; 8:28). This was the context for Paul's powerful exultation and prophetic teaching regarding the imminent emergence, even now appearing, of a radically new life. Although Romans 8 does not represent classic apocalyptic literature, it assumes the apocalyptic worldview and gives voice to the spirit of those who trust it in order to find meaning and hope in the midst of crisis.

APOCALYPTIC THOUGHT AND PAUL'S MINISTRY TO THE CHURCH AT ROME

• What outcome did Paul expect from the suffering that Jesus and the early Christians endured? (Read Romans 8:21, 29.) How were his hopes realized or disappointed?
• What evidence do you see that certain segments of society today expect a great conflict between good and evil? Do those expecting the end of history as we know it look forward to it eagerly as the fulfillment of God's good purpose, or do they approach it with fear? Why?
• As you anticipate the inevitable major changes of a new millennium, how do you feel? How does the gospel Paul proclaimed address your feelings and thoughts? (Read Romans 8:18, 37-39.)

IN CLOSING

• What are the most significant marks of the Spirit for you? How does the presence of the Holy Spirit empower and guide you? make you feel? How does the power of the Spirit help you to endure suffering and overcome the tragedies and difficulties of life?
• Commit some time to prayer for those who truly suffer (as well as for those who complain about inconvenience but do not know real suffering). Ponder how the acceptance of Jesus Christ as Savior and Redeemer and God's gracious gift of the Spirit has enriched and transformed your life. Take time in prayer, if the Spirit leads you, to make or to reaffirm that acceptance.

---

[1] From *Two Types of Faith*, by Martin Buber (Routledge & Kegan Paul Ltd., 1951).

V THE SOVEREIGNTY OF GOD

The Called and the Chosen
Read Romans 9

According to Luke, writing in Acts, the apostle Paul was warned repeatedly while he was on his way to Jerusalem with the offering for the mother church that he would face severe difficulty there that might cost him his life (Acts 21:4, 7-14). Paul's opponents would charge him with polluting the Temple and teaching against the observance of the Law (Acts 21:21, 27-28; compare Galatians 3:23-29). Paul had anticipated these dangers. He was aware of the risk he took in making his way to Jerusalem before going on to Rome (Romans 15:30-32). Conflicts had arisen with the Judaizers early in his work and also with the apostle Peter (Galatians 2:4-5, 11-14). As early as the A.D. 50's, Paul was being accused of betrayal of the Jewish tradition. Now, as he wrote to the Christian community at Rome, he wrestled inwardly with these charges and declared openly his profound love for his fellow Jews. He did not deserve the cruel conspiracy to destroy him that was developing. Moreover, as a devout Jew from birth, the now mature Paul ached for the salvation of his "kindred according to the flesh" (Romans 9:3).

Paul, identifying with the great prophet Moses making intercession for the idolatrous Israelites (see Exodus

32:30-34 for the story of the golden calf), wished that he could lay down his own salvation for the sake of his people. Paul would sacrifice his relationship with God if that would result in the salvation of his fellow Jews. All this formed a background for the apostle's theological declaration in Chapter 11, as well as his seemingly overstated declaration of his utter sincerity in Romans 9:1: "I am speaking the truth in Christ—I am not lying; my conscience confirms it by the Holy Spirit."

The personal and political aspects of the debate over Paul's doctrine helped to forge a theological platform for discussion. This platform rose above questions of heresy and apostasy or petty infighting to the question of the integrity and sovereignty of God and a clarification of what it means for a people to be called and chosen for salvation. In developing his platform, Paul introduced two significant terms: *promise* and *election*. The term *promise* refers to God's power intervening in history to direct the course of events, as personified in the birth through Sarah of Isaac and the birth through Rebecca of Esau and Jacob (9:9-10). Note that Hagar's son Ishmael is not considered as an heir even though he was Abraham's son, because he was not the result of God's word and miraculous intervention.

The term *election* refers to God's having selected the nation of Israel through the descendants of Abraham and Sarah to perform a critical task in the unfolding drama of God's saving purpose (9:11-12). Paul's point is that one does not gain salvation through one's own choice or personal righteousness but by way of God's authority to save.

In so arguing, Paul treads a dangerously thin line between portraying God as having ultimate authority to direct the course of history and being a whimsical despot like the pagan gods whom the Gentiles had feared from time immemorial (see 9:15 and 9:18). Sensing the rhetorical risk he has taken in defense of God's sovereignty, Paul reintroduces the diatribe beginning with Romans 9:19. The straw man asks the question Paul wants to answer: "Why then does he still find fault? For who can resist his will?" Paul responds by using the analogy of the potter and the clay (9:21). His point is that human reason as a means of understanding God leads to impudence and is entirely inadequate for the pursuit of truth. Humankind can never comprehend the complexity and breadth of God's will and purpose, nor should any of us challenge God's authority.

It is here that Paul distinguishes between being a descendant of Abraham and one chosen and called to be an heir of the promises of God to Abraham. The key is righteousness by faith, not by ethnicity or a disciplined lifestyle defined by observance of a particular code of conduct. Both Jews and Gentiles are given the opportunity to believe and through faith to live according to God's will (9:24, 30-32). Those who do will comprise the remnant with whom God has prepared to share God's glory (9:27). All this proves in dramatic proportions that we, the creatures, cannot control the Creator; rather, we depend upon the Creator's goodwill.

Paul slips from a rather austere and philosophical discussion of righteousness that comes by faith rather than by law into a highly symbolic and midrashic use of Isaiah 28:16 and 8:14-15 in Romans 9:33. This prepares the careful reader for what will follow in Romans 10:6-13. This swift and subtle shift from a generic discussion of righteousness to a highly specific claim that one must publicly profess Jesus as Lord in order to be saved deserves examination. Earlier in Paul's letter, his focus was on the "faith that was in Jesus." Now he moves into faith in Jesus as Lord as if there was no real difference.

Paul quotes from two prophetic passages that use the imagery of a stone. In Isaiah 28, the stone is a foundation stone of justice and righteousness, based on the keeping of the law and exercising fair judgment based on the law. To live by God's law is to trust God's righteous judgment, that is, God's justice. In Isaiah 8:14-15, the stone is something that causes people to stumble. It seems that Paul takes both meanings to his reference to the stone in Romans 9:33. God has given Jesus, crucified and risen, to humankind. Those who trust God's goodness will receive him by faith. Those who cannot will fall by the wayside.

Plainly put, Paul wrestles with the paradox between God's justice and God's mercy in his argument that God can be trusted. Paul asserts that God never breaks promises. God is always at work for the salvation of the world through the chosen people. God never gives up on those whom God "knows" and loves; yet, at the same time, God will ultimately demonstrate God's own righteousness by condemning those who reject Jesus as Savior and Lord (Romans 10:5-13).

THE CALLED AND THE CHOSEN

• Read Romans 9:1-5. What is it like to be profoundly misinterpreted and reproached by people you love, as Paul was? Have you ever found yourself in a controversial position that led you to divide your world between those who agree with you and those who do not, as Paul did when he continually thought of the world as made up of Jews and Gentiles? How might this kind of division actually contribute to further misunderstanding and alienation in your own community? If you were to sit down for Bible study with a Jew in your town and focus on Romans 9, what might the result be? Why?

> • Read Romans 9:6-18; compare Exodus 9:16. How do you feel and think about a God who raises up a Pharaoh (or perhaps a Hitler or a Milosevic) "for the very purpose of showing [his] power"? Has God hardened the hearts of the people who do not believe in Jesus as Lord? Why or why not?
> • Read Romans 9:19-33. Paul comments on resistance to and "stumbling" over belief in Jesus Christ as the Messiah. What did Paul see as the consequences of this resistance? Might there be significant new insights that we resist because they do not fit into our understanding of reality, just as the Jews could not accept a dying and rising Messiah? Explain.

The Christian Confession of Faith
Read Romans 10

When Paul addressed his "brothers and sisters" (Gentile and Jewish-Christian believers) at Rome a second time regarding his love for the Jews (see 9:31 and 10:1), Paul clearly set himself apart from those of his religious and ethnic heritage. When he asserted that he prayed for "them" passionately that "they may be saved" (Romans 10:1-2), Paul apparently saw himself as over-against those who were as yet unenlightened. He felt divided and saw the world's people as divided, not so much between Jew and Gentile, but as between those who believe in Jesus Christ and those who do not. He could not compromise his ultimate allegiance to the risen Christ revealed to him as Lord. Paul understood himself to be "enlightened" and his fellow Jews to be blind and stubbornly resistant (10:21). He claimed that Christ is the fulfillment or completion of the Law (10:4). All of the Law and the Prophets should have prepared the Jews to receive Jesus as Messiah, but they could not see him as he is.

Paul insisted that to believe in Jesus Christ is not difficult. Doing so does not require a flight into the heavens or into some abyss. No ecstatic or profound initiation is necessary (10:6-7; compare Deuteronomy 30:11-14). One need only accept and believe the truth from the depths of one's self and then confess publicly that Jesus is Lord. Therefore, anyone, Jew or Gentile, can be saved.

Paul offered no explanation, at this point, of what he meant by the term *saved* (Romans 10:1). In this section of his letter, the term seems static, as if it is once and for all time accomplished by way of recognizing the Christ through faith and making a public statement to that effect (10:4). The content of salvation as he understood it, however, can easily be gleaned from his earlier discussion of righteousness. *Righteousness*, as Paul used the term, was synonymous with the forensic term *justification*. That is to say, Paul understood the believer to be accounted innocent of transgression against the law upon having believed "through faith in Jesus Christ" (3:22).

In the context of the entire letter, most scholars believe that Paul conceived of salvation as a process that begins when one hears and believes the gospel. It continues through a lifetime of obedience and sanctification by God's Word and Holy Spirit and reaches fulfillment beyond mortal life in eternal communion with God. The term used in Romans 10:9, 13, rightly understood, refers, therefore, to an eschatological event that unfolds over the course of eternity, beginning with persons hearing the gospel and receiving it by faith.

Having declared so openly his understanding of the Christian confession of faith, Paul asked how Jews were to know and receive the gospel unless it was preached to them (Romans 10:14-17). The question is honest but rhetorical at the same time. Paul must have thoughtfully and prayerfully examined his own method of teaching and preaching in the synagogues, wondering what he could do differently to communicate more effectively. At the same time, he was convinced, particularly from his study of the suffering servant psalms of Isaiah, that his fellow Jews should know and recognize Jesus, based on their own study of the Scriptures and the teaching they received in the synagogue schools. He despairs that they do not (10:18-20). Yet, to comfort himself, perhaps, he quotes Isaiah speaking for God: "All day long I have held out my hands to a disobedient and contrary people" (Romans 10:21). Paul has done what he can.

THE CHRISTIAN CONFESSION OF FAITH

• Read Romans 10:1-4, 18-21. Paul evidently felt some sense of alienation from other Jews. What is it like to feel that you are closer to people not related to you genetically or culturally than to those who are? What are the consequences? How do you feel about Paul's frustration and spiritual anguish in being unable to convey his faith experience to his fellow Jews? Have you ever been in a similar position when trying to share faith with someone you love? If so, how do you deal with the fact that you cannot bring someone you care about into the faith you value so much?

• What does Paul mean that the Jews are "not enlightened"? What would they have to be or do to find enlightenment?

• Read Romans 10:5-17. Do you know of people who believe and teach that a person has to have a particular religious experience in order to be saved? If so, do you agree or disagree? Why? Had Paul had a particular religious experience that enabled him to believe in a way that his Jewish kindred could not?

The Kindness and the Severity of God: An Imponderable Wisdom
Read Romans 11

Paul asserted that in spite of the apparent rejection of Jesus by Israel, there were among the Jews a significant number of people who remained faithful to their God.

Paul was, after all, a case in point (Romans 11:1). Even among those who have refused the gospel, there are those who, in the end, will be given the gift of faith by grace. God, who called and chose the Jewish people to receive their Messiah, will preserve a remnant prepared to receive that greatest of all gifts (11:2-5). Paul could be confident of this because he knew God to be trustworthy and faithful to fulfill the calling of God's chosen people, whom God "foreknew" and loved (11:2).

The grace of which Paul wrote in Romans 10:6 was deeply informed by his own personal experience of undeserved revelation on the road to Damascus. God's grace toward him who had stubbornly rejected the gospel until that critical day would be extended in the end to all the faithful Jews when Christ would be revealed to them also (compare 11:1; Philippians 2:9-11). Nevertheless, this remnant must not be confused with all the descendants of Abraham or with the entire nation of Israel, for not all Jews are among the "elect." However, some Jews had already received the gospel and been counted among the believers throughout the Roman Empire, proving that they were also among the "elect" or those selected for the righteousness that comes by faith (Romans 11:7).

Moreover, God will use even the current unbelief of the faithful Jews as a means of bringing about the fulfillment of the Abrahamic covenant: "In you all the families of the earth shall be blessed" (Genesis 12:3). Because of them the Gentiles will be saved. That is, the gospel will be preached throughout the known world by evangelists and teachers who, wearied by their unfruitful work in the synagogues, have fanned out into the city streets and small communities of the entire Roman Empire.

Paul envisioned his kindred in the flesh (his fellow

Jews) becoming jealous of the well-being and fulfillment present among Christians who had found a right and joyful relationship with God that far outshone theirs. Paul anticipated that their jealousy would lead to their conversion and to a greater good, therefore, than might have ensued had they readily accepted the gospel when it was first offered to them. He referred to that higher good as being "life from the dead" (Romans 11:15). This phrase probably anticipates the day of the Lord when the dead will be raised incorruptible and will share in eternal communion with God. In other words, the remnant of the Jews will behold the Christ at the close of history and receive him as Messiah.

Paul then resorted to a metaphor to point beyond his apocalyptic hope to the internal validity of that hope. He referred to the bread offered in the Temple as a part of the offering of "first fruits." Just as the Jews who have believed during the initial proclamation of the gospel (the "first fruits") are counted righteous by God, so those Jews who come to believe in the end (the "root" and "branches") will also be counted righteous, for they are of the same source (Romans 11:16a). This analogy to the root of a tree and its branches may be a reference to the stump of Jesse (see Isaiah 11:1).

This powerful allusion to God's promised Messiah as coming forth from the destruction of Israel inspired hope in the apostle for his beloved people. Surely God's people are holy to the Lord in spite of their current unbelief, especially in that God had stricken them with this spiritual sluggishness and would not condemn them for something they could not help (Romans 11:7-10).

Having satisfied himself and, he hopes, his readers, with a clear affirmation of God's steadfast love and mercy toward the chosen people, Paul then underscored the Gentiles' need to respect their unbelieving Jewish neighbors and to avoid becoming haughty about their status with God. Paul used the tree as a metaphor for the people of God (11:17-19), drawing from numerous passages from the Prophets (see Isaiah 61:3; Jeremiah 11:16-17). The branches that are broken off are the unbelieving Jews. The branches grafted in, of course, are the Gentile Christians. The Gentiles are to remember that their faith derives from that of the Jews (Romans 11:18). In a flash of irony, both Jew and Gentile reader would understand the image of grafting a "wild olive shoot" (the Gentiles) into cultured stock, or "the rich root" (the Jewish tradition): a reversal of accepted agricultural practice (11:17). The appropriate response of the Gentile believer to the grace of God, therefore, is awe, not pride (11:20c).

Again Paul found it necessary to hold the justice and the mercy of God in dynamic tension. Neither could be sacrificed in an adequate theology and spiritual life. In so doing, Paul referred to "the kindness and the severity of God" (Romans 11:22). This brief remark corrects any assumption that some might make that this section of Romans proclaims universal salvation for all in the end. Paul asserts that no matter what one's confession of faith or religious heritage, one must remain submissive and obedient toward the God who has revealed the way of salvation through Jesus Christ. Persons can be as easily cut off from the people of God as they have been grafted in. We must not become too confident lest we lose our appreciation and respect for the gift we have received by grace through faith (11:23-24).

Romans 11:25-32 reasserts what has been developed in Chapters 9–11 and functions as a summary statement.

Although these verses could be read out of context as a statement that all the genetic descendants of Abraham will be saved in the end (11:26a, 32), this could not have been Paul's belief (recall 11:7-10). He would not contradict himself within the same section of his manuscript. Having reached his conclusion on the important topic of the Jews' relationship with God in light of the gospel, Paul nevertheless recognized that he had extended himself beyond the realm of reason and beyond the measure of his own spiritual insight. Much of what he longed to know remained a mystery that God alone comprehends (11:33-35). Nonetheless, Paul felt his own faith confirmed and his argument secured by the "inscrutability" of God as he moved out of the realm of rhetoric into the realm of worship with his exaltation, "For from him and through him and to him are all things. To him be the glory forever. Amen" (Romans 11:36; see 1 Corinthians 8:6).

THE KINDNESS AND THE SEVERITY OF GOD

• Read Romans 11:1-10. How does Paul understand the concept of the remnant? What will this mean for the Jews, according to Paul?
• Do you know someone who simply cannot believe in God, no matter how much he or she wishes he or she could, but is at the same time one of the most humane and generous people anyone would hope to meet? Can you relate your own experiences to Paul's resolution of the problem of the salvation of his fellow Jews?
• Why, do you think, do some persons find it easy, when others find it difficult or impossible, to believe in the promises of God? Would anyone be jealous of the joyful, loving faith that you and your community demonstrate by faith in Jesus Christ? Might your example lead anyone to want to share your faith?
• Read Romans 11:11-24. Examine the analogy of the grafting and the branches. What analogy or image might you use now to describe the process of integration and union of various persons into the

fold of Christianity? Are you aware of anti-Semitism in your community
or of feelings of superiority between one Christian congregation and
another? What spiritual danger might exist when such feelings persist?
How might you and your group work to transform pride into awe and
respect both for others who seek God and for the mystery of God's saving work? What might cause a believer to be "cut off" from God?
• Read Romans 11:25-36. Do you believe that God will condemn anyone permanently? that all will be saved, regardless of how they have
lived their lives? What does Paul's teaching suggest?

The Jewish Remnant

A perplexing debate lingers on regarding Paul's
thought and teaching about God's sovereignty over the
salvation of the Jews and the necessity of the Christian
confession of faith. The question that continues to be
asked is, "Did Paul believe that the faithful Jewish remnant would have to acknowledge Jesus as Messiah in
order to be saved?" Within the context of Chapters 9–11,
in which Paul dealt with this subject, it seems that he does
expect them to recognize and believe in Christ at the conclusion of history. A close examination of the final verses
of that section, however, reveals that Paul does not specifically state that his kinsmen in the flesh will be saved
through faith in Jesus as the Christ. Salvation will be a
matter of the elimination of sin from Jacob. They will be
saved, not because of their faith, but out of God's faithfulness to their ancestors. God will save them as an act of
divine mercy (Romans 11:25-32). This debate is important, of course, because of the continuing relevance of
interfaith dialogue and harmony between Jews and
Christians. The fact that Paul leaves the resolution of the
issue to God, the source and goal of all life, suggests that
contemporary inter-faith dialogue should remain open and

respectful of the integrity of Jews even though they do
not accept Jesus as Messiah.

THE JEWISH REMNANT

• How can you be involved in inter-faith dialogue in your community?
Is it appropriate, do you think, for Christians of any denomination to
attempt to convert, proselytize, or evangelize Jews or persons of other
religious traditions if they are not open or willing to listen? If conversion
or evangelization is not the point of inter-faith dialogue, what is?

IN CLOSING

• Summarize your insights on the sovereignty of God. What does that
mean for you? How do you identify the called and the chosen? What
do you do, if anything, about those who do not care to be called or
chosen?
• Join in prayer for inter-faith dialogue and for the integrity and appreciation of the diversity within the kingdom of God. Reflect on how Jesus
Christ is the Savior to all, and take time to renew or make a commitment to follow him in faith.

VI THE PRACTICE OF THE GOSPEL IN COMMUNITY LIFE

The Transformed People
Read Romans 12

· Chapter 12 to end

With the "Amen" at the close of Romans 11, Paul's theological dissertation comes to a close. In the remaining sections of his letter to the church at Rome, Paul seeks to guide the believers into the practical application of the gospel. Just as the focus of Paul's understanding of God's saving work through Jesus was not on the salvation of the individual, so also the focus of his practical theology is not on the individual but on the community. Each exhortation refers primarily to the logic of community life in the Spirit rather than to private moral responsibility before God.

Having led his readers into a more profound awareness of God as the source and the goal of existence, through whom believers receive salvation as an act of mercy, Paul asks the congregations at Rome to consecrate their entire selves to the service of God as their fundamental act of worship. The religious practices of the new faith are not to be matters of ritual or dogma but, rather, primarily matters of ethics in interpersonal relationships.

Acknowledging the mystery of God, believers are to live in full submission and respect for their dependence upon God's guidance of their common life. Christian living is to be sacramental at its core. Every decision is to be tested by the Spirit who dwells within the community of believers. In this way the choices and responses the church makes in its everyday functioning may reflect the will of God. The community's values, judgments, thought processes, and procedures are not to emerge from patterns set by the pagan or secular environment in which they live but from their knowledge of God by the Spirit (Romans 12:1-2).

While the Hellenistic philosophical culture called for excelling above one's peers in the classic virtues, Paul's teaching called for humility and service to the needs and functions required by the new community of believers (12:3-5). Inasmuch as all believers who truly belonged to Christ partook of the same Spirit, all were gifted for a particular aspect of the work required for harmony in the community (8:9; 12:6-8). Each member, therefore, was to exercise his or her gift out of respect for its source and for its importance to the well-being of the entire community. At the same time, every individual member needed to serve as his or her own judge in estimating the value of his or her service, based on the amount of faith being exercised in the ministry performed (12:3). The greater respect should always be given to those who fulfill their function in simplicity and generosity out of a heartfelt trust in the faith of Jesus.

Paul was fond of using the human body as an analogy for the Christian community (12:4-5; 1 Corinthians 12:12-27). Undoubtedly he understood the body to be governed by the head and expected that his readers would understand his analogy to the mind of Christ guiding the community of believers. The metaphor worked well for Paul because he understood the church to be a dynamic organism with well-ordered systems, each of which has a vital role in the healthy functioning of the entire unit. Each gift and each ministry, no matter how seemingly ordinary, such as giving, should be regarded as being as important as the functions that attract the greater attention, such as prophecy or miracles. Moreover, each of the believers belongs, not to herself or himself as a free agent, but to the body as a whole and ultimately to Christ (Romans 12:5).

The list of charismata or spiritual gifts found in Romans 12:6-8, when compared with the list in 1 Corinthians 12, is relatively short. Apparently Paul wrote to the community at Rome with the understanding that the spiritual gifts were fully operational there but were not being used in excess or in a disorderly manner. In other words, the church at Rome was not to be characterized by its exercise of spiritual gifts, necessarily, as was the clearly charismatic community at Corinth. Paul's list of gifts in Romans 12:6-8 is designed only to create the occasion to exhort the readers to utilize the gifts by faith for the purpose of serving generously, diligently, and cheerfully.

A clear understanding of the ministry functions that Paul named, however, may help the modern-day reader to focus on ministries that Paul found to be most visible and particularly vulnerable to misuse. The ministry of inspired speech (prophecy) could easily be counterfeited or compromised, as Paul knew too well from his experiences in Corinth, for example. Heresy and divisiveness were common. Every inspired utterance needed to be tested by those exercising the ministry of discernment (see 1 Corinthians 14:1-19).

The term *ministry* (*diakonia*) referred to any work of service to the community, including teaching. The order of deacon received its name from this term (see Romans 16:1). In Phoebe's case, her diaconal role probably included serving as a <u>benefactor</u> and a <u>financial officer</u> for Paul, the missionary evangelist. The <u>teacher's</u> role was to train as accurately and thoroughly as possible new converts in the faith handed down to them through the apostles. The exhorter was to provide moral and spiritual instruction, <u>guidance</u>, and encouragement. The <u>giver</u> supported the community financially. Those more able to give were to do so freely, and those less able to give were to do so with trust in God's provision for them. The <u>leader</u> exercised governance but was not to dominate or <u>control</u>. The <u>com-</u> <u>passionate</u> served the needs of the poor, the orphans, and the widows. They were not to exercise their ministry as a burdensome duty or as a service for which they were to be honored but as a glad response to the compassion they had received from God. A congregation or community that is highly gifted can become overly confident and proud. Paul urged the churches at Rome to <u>take on a ser-</u> <u>vant's mentality</u>.

   <u>Paul the theologian</u> became <u>Paul the exhorter</u> as he wrote Romans 12:9-21. The <u>preacher of the gospel</u> became the <u>encourager</u> giving moral instruction to the community of faith. Although Paul rarely quoted from the sayings of Jesus in his writings, this series of proverbial sayings seems to reflect the influence of Jesus' teaching found in the Q material (source material for some of the Gospels) or in the Sermon on the Mount. Note that the instructions are given to the community rather than to individuals. The underlying theme is mutual love and the pursuit of peace through non-resistance and prayer. Humility and keeping company with the "lowly" are urged, along with showing "hospitality to strangers" (probably traveling Christians). This section of Paul's practical theology foreshadows his further exhortation in Romans 13:8-10.

source that has disappeared

THE TRANSFORMED PEOPLE

• Read Romans 12:1-7. How does Paul define spiritual worship? How does your faith community define and practice it? Are the two definitions different and, if so, why?

• Paul admonished the first-century Roman Christians not to be "conformed to this world." What aspects of the secular culture in Rome might have been present within the churches at Rome? (Refer back to Chapter I, if necessary.) How might the popular culture and values of post-modern society influence your church in a way that Paul would challenge? *self-serving*

• How effectively *minimal* does your faith community acknowledge the spiritual gifts and ministry functions of its members? What might you do to help others recognize and develop a faithful practice of ministry?

• Read Romans 12:9-21. What are the marks of the Christian community? How might this list of characteristics inform your own church? help it manage conflict? help it grow? *Recognition of all contributions; opportunity for diversity; promotion of other than a single agenda — ie "I have all the answers."*

The Church and Civil Authorities
Read Romans 13:1-7

Under the Roman government, the rule of law was first practiced in a manner that could sustain peace for an extended period of time. It was this system of law and order that would lead Paul to seek justice in Rome when he was arrested in Jerusalem at the hands of an angry mob. It had allowed him on occasions prior to that, when mistreated by local authorities, to appeal to his Roman citizenship in order to be treated fairly. It was the Roman Peace that allowed for the free proclamation and swift spread of the gospel throughout the western Mediterranean region under his and other Christian ministers' oversight. Under Roman law, the Jews, and by extension, the early Christians, had a certain religious freedom, which limited the potential conflict between the Christian movement and the governmental authorities. All these factors influenced Paul's positive valuation of civil authority.

Paul was eager to maintain a good reputation for the Christian movement in Rome and beyond Rome in order that their life might prosper and his work might continue unhindered. His instruction to the members of the communities at Rome to pay taxes and to respect and honor those in authority paralleled Jesus' words when he instructed his followers to pay to Caesar the things that belong to Caesar and to God the things that belong to God (Mark 12:17).

Many read Romans 13:1-7 as social conservatism, believing that true Christianity automatically challenges the injustices of established power. The evidence indicates, however, that early Christianity relied heavily on the established authorities for its success and functioned primarily as a reform movement within Jewish religion and as a path to salvation for those seeking God. Early Christianity never understood itself as a social revolution, though its values planted the seeds for major changes in the status of slaves and women, for example, and threatened the economies of some communities that depended upon pagan worship and sexual excesses.

THE CHURCH AND CIVIL AUTHORITIES

• Read Romans 13:1-7. Why was the Christian movement of the first century not a social reform or social justice movement? Remember to consider the widespread expectation that Christ would soon return.

Trying to deal w/ a new concept of God thru Jesus; of individual commitment + responsibility

The Christian Ethic Summarized
and Further Exhortations
Read Romans 13:8-14

Paul shifts from his call to submit to civil authority to a parallel call to obey divine authority. Just as the Christian community is to give the Roman authorities all that it "owes" them ("owe" and "due" are the same word in Greek; see Romans 13:7), so it must be in debt to no one else. More positively, the Christian community is to see itself as owing others, regardless of their position in society, the respect and love that God's law requires. Just as Jesus completes the Law and the Prophets, making the revelation of God's salvation plainly available to all, so the Christians' love for one another will reveal the goal of the Law and Prophets as having been reached (13:8-10). In this teaching, Paul passes down to the church at Rome the very teaching of Jesus as recorded in the Synoptic Gospels (see Matthew 22:37-39; Mark 12:29-31; Luke 10:27).

Paul next resorted to the eschatological hope of the early church in order to inspire a sense of urgency about rejecting the patterns of the pagan world and practicing the new life that the believer takes on in baptism (Romans 13:11-14). The apostle reclaimed his hope that God would soon bring to fulfillment the hope to which he had referred in Romans 8:19: "the revealing of the children of God." The references to laying aside and putting on reflect a common metaphor of changing clothes as an image of replacing vices with virtues. In addition, early Christian converts changed from street clothes into baptismal garments for the sacrament. In baptism, the believer dies and rises with Christ into a new life, having rejected the stan-

dards of the life of sin and having been "transformed by
the renewing of [his or her] mind" (see Romans 6:1-11;
12:2). In all of this exhortation, Paul reinforced the many
sayings of Jesus that called for alertness as the day of the
Lord approached (see Luke 21:34-36).

THE CHRISTIAN ETHIC SUMMARIZED

• Read Romans 13:8-14. What does it mean today "to put on the Lord
Jesus Christ"? How does your baptism call you to the life of Christ that
Paul describes in this passage? *Practice his example*

The Weak and the Strong:
Hospitality of Heart and Behavior
Read Romans 14:1–15:13

When Paul addressed the strong within the Christian
community, he very likely addressed the higher nature of
all his readers, hoping that everyone would identify with
the strong and choose to follow the pattern he described
as that of the strong among them (Romans 14:1; 15:1). At
the same time, his letter to the church at Rome was primarily addressed to Gentile Christians who were in the
majority. Paul's purpose was at least twofold. First, he
wanted to encourage a non-judgmental attitude toward
people whose practices and preferences were different.
Second, he wanted to serve as an agent of reconciliation
between the Gentile Christians who had become dominant
in the Christian house churches in Rome over the previous
decade and the Jewish Christians who were returning
from exile and seeking full participation in the Christian
community. Paul clearly believed that Christ was the completion of the law and, therefore, believers need no longer

not sure where they were.

follow Jewish sabbath and food laws. Nevertheless, the ethnic Jews within the Christian community very likely preferred to maintain their Jewish practices even as they developed their faith in Christ. Paul's point is that God will save or condemn. The Christian community's responsibility is to welcome any seeker after God in love and respect (Romans 14:4-5; compare Matthew 7:1-2; 15:11).

Paul taught that the freedom enjoyed by the believer because of Christ was not to lead to individualism but should be used in service of the community. True liberty lay in the pursuit of the well-being of the whole (Romans 14:13; 15:2). Paul illustrated his point by a lengthy discussion of table practices and eating meat (14:13-23), but his exhortation was not focused on resolving the issue of diet. Rather, he focused on encouraging "righteousness and peace and joy in the Holy Spirit" (14:17). Paul's goal was that every decision made by an individual or a particular house church would lead to the edification of all the believers and to increasing harmony (14:19).

Having made his primary point plainly, Paul retreated to the more generic matter of the individual Christian conscience (Romans 14:22-23). Ultimately, every person must stand before God the Judge. In order to live at peace with one's God as well as with one's self, each believer must be confident that what he or she does is in harmony with the word and will of God. Stated more positively, every individual act must be an act of faith, no matter how minor the deed or decision may be; "for whatever does not proceed from faith is sin" (14:23). That almost incidental conclusion crystallizes Paul's teaching that righteousness is a matter of faith and not of observing the law, even in the smallest matters of everyday life.

Ultimately, Paul's exhortations regarding the hospitality

to be practiced toward the weak by the strong in faith all derive from the example of Christ Jesus (15:3). According to Paul's spirituality, Christ Jesus "emptied himself, / taking the form of a slave" (Philippians 2:7). The important thing about the welcoming nature of the truly Christian community is that the church might glorify or honor God who has offered grace, not judgment, toward all who believe: "Welcome one another, therefore, just as Christ has welcomed you, for the glory of God" (Romans 15:7).

Those who had had no claim to the knowledge of God or a relationship with the God of the Jews, that is, the Gentiles, have been received openly (15:8-12). Note how Paul has, throughout his letter, frequently quoted from Deuteronomy, from certain key psalms, and from the prophet Isaiah. Paul was eager to demonstrate that the gospel his Gentile readers received so freely came as the fulfillment of God's relationship with the Jews. Jesus was, first of all, God's promised Messiah for the Jews and only afterward Savior for the world. Again, Paul's pastoral purpose was to heighten the respect that the Gentile Christians showed their Jewish Christian brothers and sisters within the church at Rome.

Paul's benediction at the close of his exhortation focused on the gift of hope provided the Gentiles and the joy with which they were to receive it. That joy was to be experienced by way of the "power of the Holy Spirit" (15:13). In the end, Paul knew that no amount of thought or discipline could evoke the winsome, generous, and humble spirit he hoped to find in the community at Rome. This would be the work of a power beyond human strength, the fruit of the indwelling Holy Spirit. This joyful hospitality would be the gospel demonstrated with signs and wonders, not in the form of supernatural occurrences, but in the form of renewed minds and transformed relationships of faithful love (1:16-17; 12:2; compare 15:18-19).

THE WEAK AND THE STRONG

[handwritten: In or out of the faith]

• Read Romans 14. Who were the weak and who were the strong in Rome, as Paul understood them? How did Paul understand how all would be accountable to God? *[handwritten: how on earth; God ultimately]*

• What does the passage about stumbling blocks and hindrances mean (14:13-23)? How does the behavior of the individual influence the whole community and other individual members? What sort of personal accountability should the Christian community demand of individual members, and how would that accountability be measured and administered? *[handwritten: Are all actions fulfilled in good for everyone.]*

• How do matters of individual liberty and social cohesion influence your congregation today? Consider matters of dress, lifestyle, musical preferences, economics, and education. Consider theological differences within your denomination. What difference does it make how people of different beliefs and practices treat one another?

[handwritten: Non-acceptance still exists (gays). Some becoming more one-dimensional. Need for tolerance + acceptance of diversity of belief.]

A Personal Addendum: Paul's Need for Support
Read Romans 15:14-33

Paul believed it appropriate to explain why it was necessary not only to give a thorough account of the gospel but also to include a lengthy exhortation to a church that, by reputation, was orderly and well equipped to instruct others. He felt a slight need to apologize for his boldness, especially in that he had no direct knowledge of their pastoral needs. Paul explained that, as the apostle to the Gentiles, he needed to be able to present the fruit of his life's work to God, confident of its purity (Romans 15:14-16). In the back of his mind, he was also preparing to give an accounting of his work to the church at Jerusalem—when he presented the collection for the poor

that he had been raising throughout the Gentile world
(15:25). Again he emphasized that no amount of diligence
or correct instruction from him as a minister of the gospel
could have resulted in the rapid spread of the Christian
movement from Jerusalem and Antioch to Illyricum (the
modern-day former Yugoslavia). This was a sign and a
wonder wrought by Christ. Christ accomplished it
through him; so when Paul boasted of the success of the
endeavor, he glorified Christ (15:18-19). Paul did not
claim to have founded all the congregations that existed at
the time among the Gentiles. Obviously an apostolic mission had preceded him to Rome (16:7). Paul only claimed
to have limited his own mission to areas that had not previously heard the gospel (15:20). Nonetheless, he felt
obliged to serve all the Gentile congregations in a supervi-
sory manner.

Paul then explained his delay in traveling to visit the
congregations at Rome, important as they were. He had
exhausted his opportunity to evangelize to the east of
Rome (15:23). He was probably referring to the urban
areas where Greek was spoken and, thus, where he could
be most effective. Paul suggests that all these areas had
mission congregations, except where the gospel had been
rejected and the apostle banished.

Apparently Paul's aim had always been to reach Rome;
but now, at last, he had a definite plan first to return to
Jerusalem, then to visit the Roman congregations on his
way to Spain and the West. He longed to spend a period
of time in fellowship and teaching at Rome, more than
likely seeking to strengthen the work there as well as to
raise financial support for his further mission work (15:24,
32). He was anxious to demonstrate the gratitude of the
Gentile Christians for the gift of faith that they owed to

the Jewish Christians, especially at Jerusalem, and to avoid controversy or conflict over his reputed anti-Jewish sentiments. Paul begged for the prayers of his spiritual kin at Rome as he approached Jerusalem boldly (15:30-32). His final prayer for himself and for the church was for the presence of the God of peace (15:33).

A PERSONAL ADDENDUM: PAUL'S NEED FOR SUPPORT

• Read Romans 15:14-33. Why, do you think, did Paul so diligently collect funds to be given to the church at Jerusalem? (Read 1 Corinthians 16:1-4; 2 Corinthians 8–9; Galatians 2:10.)
• Study a map of Paul's missionary journeys and compare it with a contemporary map of the Mediterranean basin. Find Illyricum, Rome, Macedonia, and Achaia, as well as Antioch and Jerusalem. Notice the Roman roads and sea routes Paul used in his travels.

IN CLOSING

• Summarize your insights on the Christian community in this chapter. What are the marks of the Christian community? What are your gifts? What insight or guidance comes from your Christian community in terms of what your gifts are and how they can best be used?
• Pray for all Christian communities to have Christlike harmony and unity in the midst of their differences. Pray in particular for all those persons who propagate or who suffer violence for the sake of their religion. Reflect on the gifts God has given you, and take time in prayer to make or reaffirm you commitment to love and serve Jesus Christ.

VII THE CHURCH DYNAMIC: THEN AND NOW

The Role of Women in the Church at Rome
Read Romans 16:1-16

T he urban centers of the Roman Empire and thus the congregations Paul organized were made up of people from a wide spectrum of ethnic backgrounds. Like the twenty-first century, the first century was a period of multicultural exchange, encouraged by ease of travel, a common business language, prosperity, political peace, the rule of law, and remarkable individual liberty. This diversity was reflected in the networking Paul did in fostering the Christian movement and in his references listed in Romans 16.

The motif Paul used for giving his references was his request that the readers give his personal greetings to his friends who would remember him well from other settings but who currently lived, worked, and worshiped in the congregations at Rome. The majority of the people he named as references had held positions of influence in their congregations of origin. Christianity enjoyed a limited (and inconsistent) freedom from Rome. Various emperors either tolerated or persecuted the Christians, most often in and around Rome. Paul wrote this letter during a time of relative peace, which apparently allowed Christians to hold public office without submitting to emperor worship. A few of Paul's references were people of nobility and broad reputation. Seven of the references he listed were women who held office in the church and had served in ministry with Paul on a number of missions. These people had, apparently, preceded him to Rome.

Phoebe came from Cenchreae, a port to the east of Corinth on the Aegean Sea. She had a gift for ministry and served as one of Paul's financial patrons. She was being sent with the letter to the church at Rome as an emissary for Paul, with the mission of organizing in advance for his visit (16:1-2). More than likely, a part of her work was to begin a collection in support of his mission to Spain. Clearly, Paul respected and trusted her highly, not only for her generosity and loyalty but also for her administrative abilities.

Prisca, wife of Aquila, and a partner with him in the trade of tentmaking, was a fellow minister of the gospel with Paul. She and her spouse had demonstrated their faithfulness to Paul by personally protecting him when his life was in danger. They apparently were among the more prosperous Christians at Rome and hosted a congregation in their apartment (16:3-5).

Also among Paul's many female references were Mary, Persis, and the mother of Rufus. They each worked hard on behalf of the gospel and alongside the apostle. They would have been well known to the church at Rome.

Various Bible translations have rendered the apostle's name in verse 7 as either "Junias" or "Junia." The NRSV opts for the feminine form, which suggests that Paul identified a female apostle who reached Rome with the gospel in time to assist in organizing the work already underway in that city. The greater significance of this reference, however, is the fact that the term *apostle* was used in the early church to refer to a group larger than the original twelve whom Jesus had appointed.

Clearly, even though Paul had in other letters apparently limited the work of women in the churches, women contributed significantly to the leadership and the workforce of the movement. If Phoebe could be trusted with diplomacy and financial administration, not all the women in the churches Paul organized were uneducated or considered inferior or secondary. Although the apostle was a social conservative in some ways, wanting to maintain order and to avoid drawing undue attention to the movement from the authorities, he learned to appreciate and depend upon the gifts and ministries of women. Time was short. All hands were needed. This was not a time to argue over gender distinctions but a time to spread the gospel (see Galatians 3:27-29).

There were probably three house churches at Rome when Paul addressed the congregations there. One, as already noted, met in the home of his fellow tentmakers (Romans 16:3-5). A second met in the home of Aristobulus and was more than likely made up of his extended household, including servants and employees (16:10b). A third was organized around the household of Narcissus (16:11b). Some scholars suggest that the two lists in Romans 16:14-15 indicate two different house churches. In any case, A.B. DuToit, writing for *Hervormde Teologiese Studies*, interprets Paul's request that they greet one another with a holy kiss to mean that the house churches did find opportunity to meet together as one greater community (16:16).[1]

> **THE ROLE OF WOMEN IN THE CHURCH AT ROME**
>
> • Read Romans 1:1-16 and count how many women Paul mentioned. Use a Bible dictionary to look up their names and what is known about each of them. How does this respect for women compare with what you have typically been taught about Paul and women? What difference might it make to the church to recognize Junia, a woman, as one of the early apostles?

Dissenters and Supporters
Read Romans 16:17-27

Just as Paul was not specific regarding what he considered to be the issues between the weak and the strong of faith at Rome, so he is vague about the controversy he suspected existed at Rome. One might hypothesize that, having given a prodigious list of personal references and having dared to recommend Phoebe and her mission, Paul expected that some opposition to his intentions and his right to represent the Gentile mission in Spain would emerge. As an afterthought, then, Paul warns his readers not to be dissuaded from their support of him and his gospel mission by those who, in truth, serve only their own ambitions and not the Lord Jesus Christ (Romans 16:18). Paul expected that some smooth-talking leaders at Rome would attempt to lead some of the less well-trained converts to misconstrue Paul's message to and request of the church (16:18). His pastoral exhortation, "I want you to be wise in what is good and guileless in what is evil" (16:19), sounds very much like the proverb Jesus quoted: "Be wise as serpents and innocent as doves" (compare 16:19 with Matthew 10:16). Evidently, Paul was feeling attacked not simply by divisive critics, but by evil itself. His hope was that the end of Satan's rule would finally come, and God's peace would be consummated imminently (Romans 16:20a).

As was always the case, Paul worked with a team of fellow ministers, even in his correspondence with the churches. Timothy he treated as a son and soul mate. Tertius served as Paul's secretary, taking dictation. Gaius of Corinth hosted the house church where Paul was ministering at the time he wrote. There is independent evidence that Erastus held public office in the city of Corinth during the mid-first century.[2] The apostle, however, gave this letter its authority. His concluding blessing sealed the effectiveness of the letter for those who received it by faith. Paul offered up the gospel and the obedience of faith it would engender in its hearers at Rome as praise to God through Jesus Christ. Paul's only desire and full expectation was that God would be honored (16:25-27).

DISSENTERS AND SUPPORTERS

• Read Romans 17–20. Paul cautions the congregation to guard against those who would undermine their work. Recall an instance of resistance to a new idea, program, staff member, or ministry in your congregation. What positive steps were taken to understand and engage the resistance in a healthy, helpful way? What opposition and effort went "underground" and became unhealthy and harmful? How was the dissent resolved? What lessons did you learn?

The Mystery Revealed: Conclusions

The body of Paul's letter to the church at Rome represents a strategic effort on Paul's part to establish common ground between him and a community that he hoped would support his mission. His purpose was not to draft a doctrinal standard for the Gentile mission or the church universal. Rather he hoped to establish the broadest possible theological and spiritual framework, which all the

Roman believers, no matter what their ethnic background, could embrace. Moreover, he hoped to build significant depth of fellowship between him and his fellow believers at Rome in advance of his visit.

The mature missionary, facing the most difficult phase of his ministry with vision and courage, wrote the letter to the church at Rome with remarkable agility and equilibrium. This treatise addressed a number of the conflicts that had surfaced in his earlier work with a heightened level of discipline and balance. The distance he had from any internal congregational conflicts that might have existed at Rome contributed to the formal style of his correspondence with the believers there. The peace that the church at Rome apparently enjoyed at that time also contributed. The most significant factor, however, may well have been Paul's increasing wisdom. Among the issues he addressed so deftly were the tension between law and gospel, the roles of women and men in the church, the relationship between Gentile Christians and Jewish Christians, the salvation of the Jews and whether they must acknowledge Jesus as Lord, individual freedom and community harmony, and submission to civil authority in the context of willingness to suffer for the gospel. While Romans is not a systematic theology, it is the most reasoned and thorough expression of the Christian faith found in the New Testament.

THE MYSTERY REVEALED: CONCLUSIONS

• How do the creeds, Scriptures, church traditions, and your experience in the faith form the foundation for your church? How does theological diversity affect your church, and what core beliefs do you rely upon to maintain your unity of fellowship today? How does your congregation develop a clear and reasoned stance on potentially divisive matters of Christian living? How does the mature leadership of your community contribute to peaceful and responsible ethics?

Issues Resolved

The apparent juxtaposition of law and gospel in Paul's writing reflects the tension between Jewish Christians and Gentile Christians as well as Paul's own spiritual journey. Paul concluded that observing the law cannot save anyone. Therefore, it is unnecessary for Gentile believers to practice circumcision or to follow the full complement of Jewish dietary and sabbath laws. In this the apostles at Jerusalem concurred with Paul (see Acts 15; Galatians 2:1-10). The revealed law of God served, Paul taught, only to make it obvious that humans are sinners in need of redemption. The gospel makes righteousness a genuine possibility by faith and brings the work of the law and the prophets to completion and fulfillment.

All the members of the church, if they truly belong to Christ, "have the Spirit of Christ" or the Spirit of God (understood to be synonymous) within them. Thus, regardless of gender, males and females are due respect and have responsibility to exercise their ministries by faith. All are to "outdo" the other in showing love and honor (Romans 12:10). Women, as well as men, can host congregations and exercise God-appointed leadership roles in the church.

While the more liberal or freer Gentile Christians may think themselves enlightened and more advanced in faith than their Jewish Christian brothers and sisters, they must not be haughty. The freedom and faith of the Gentiles derives from the inheritance they received from the Jews. They owe a debt of gratitude and respect to their Jewish Christian brothers and sisters. In fact, they must be willing to forfeit their individual liberty in service of those who are more conservative than they are. The highest goal of Christian community shall be that the God of peace be with the believers to govern them and be honored in their fellowship.

Although the Jews have, in the main, rejected Jesus as their Messiah, God has preserved a few who will be saved. They will remain faithful to the end. God, in God's sovereignty, will extend grace sufficient to save them.

Paul may have argued that God authorized the *pax romana* (Romans 13:1), since all authorities exist only through God. Therefore the church must respect civil authority and submit to both its system of taxation and its laws. At the same time, when persecution or suffering arise (as they certainly did for the Jewish Christians in Rome prior to Paul's correspondence and for Paul in numerous towns and cities throughout the Empire), believers are to endure hardship as an act of service to God (13:2-7). They are to see their suffering as completing the suffering of Christ (8:17).

As indicated by his closing praise of God (16:25), Paul believed that God had chosen him to make plain for all to see and believe what had been hidden and unavailable to non-Jews prior to his ministry. Essentially, the mystery now revealed was that the God of Israel, who had always been at work to save the Jews, had now accomplished the salvation of the Gentiles "through the faith of Jesus." All people could now enjoy a right relationship with God as a gift offered them through Jesus who gave his life for them. They need only believe with their hearts and confess their faith openly.

The purpose of making what was secret openly available to all was to "bring about the obedience of faith" among the Gentiles (1:5; 16:26). Paul's goal was that all who believed would be made righteous through God's grace. That is, an inner attitude of generosity, hospitality, and humility derived from the unwarranted gift of the gospel itself was to characterize the worldwide Christian community.

ISSUES RESOLVED

• Which of the issues dealt with by Paul remain current issues? Why do these longstanding issues still need to be addressed when other issues have become irrelevant? Consider especially the role of women in church leadership and contemporary expressions of anti-Semitism. What are the cutting edge issues within your denomination today? How does Romans model ways of dealing with these potentially divisive concerns?

Communicating in the Vernacular

Paul was highly successful in making converts from among those of the Gentiles who preferred an enlightened monotheism to pantheism or polytheism but were familiar with the idiom of the pagan religious environment. One of Paul's major strengths was his ability and willingness to use the popular religious language of the day. By incorporating (but subordinating and transforming) the vernacular, Paul presented his gospel in both familiar and compelling terms.

In every synagogue on any sabbath throughout the Roman Empire, constituents of the synagogue, who may not have become proselytes, could be found listening to and sometimes participating directly in the prayers and songs. Otherwise known as "God-fearers," they respected the Jewish worship of one, invisible, and universal God and the high moral standards of that religion. In many cases these people would have been influenced by

Stoicism, an enlightened philosophical school enjoying revival in the second half of the first century.

Stoicism encouraged individuals to find harmony in life by discovering and practicing virtue and detachment from material things. Stoics despised self-indulgence as well as impulsive behavior. Stoicism as practiced by the average citizen philosopher, as opposed to the academic, however, often became a matter of asceticism. Paul had found this tendency even within some of his mission congregations. It could lead to despising bodily life and seeing it as something to be escaped only through death. The Stoics, to their credit, encouraged religious expression as a pursuit of harmony with the one spirit that transcends material existence. Stoics prized reason as the essence of divinity and insisted on rational religion. At the same time that many of the God-fearers would have been influenced by Stoicism, they would also have been acquainted with or were perhaps themselves converts from the widespread mystery religions of the Greek world.

The gospel that Paul preached was superior both to the newly revived Greek philosophical schools of Epicurean-ism and Stoicism and to the mystery religions in several critical ways. Instead of the individual pursuit of pleasure (as the Epicureans) or enlightenment through virtue (as the Stoics), Paul's gospel encouraged intentional Christian community and the employment of one's resources and abilities in the service of the community and the gospel. Unlike the mystery cults, his gospel required radical moral transformation and a lifestyle that excluded orgiastic activities. It imposed an internal discipline emerging out of a deep love for the moral God of Israel.

Challenging the often corrupt forms of Epicureanism, Stoicism, and goddess worship, Paul taught that the human body was the dwelling place of God in the Spirit and therefore was to be cared for as holy rather than to be indulged, debased, denied, tolerated, or despised. While in the mystery religions salvation was available only to the initiates who could afford to participate in the rites, in the church salvation was available to all. Instead of a closed society as in the mystery cults or a society of the elite as in the philosophical schools, Christianity, under Paul's influence, created an open society that had the potential of eliminating class and gender boundaries. Paul's gospel represented a step in the process of the evolution of religion.

As with all Hellenistic religion and philosophy, the goal of the spirituality Paul taught was to become like the highest ideal or like God, that is, goodness personified. In this case, to be a believer was to seek to become like Christ. Becoming like Christ, however, from Paul's point of view, had nothing to do with following the Nazarene, the itinerant teacher of Galilee. Becoming like Christ was to be achieved, instead, by faith.

Faith was a matter of identifying one's self with Jesus in his death and in his resurrection. This experience of dying and rising with Christ was not, however, mysticism in the classic sense of union with God in a non-corporeal state. Paul believed in the essential unity of the human person and anticipated a bodily resurrection at the end of history. Therefore, the believer would follow a discipline during his or her mortal life that emphasized sanctification and the indwelling Holy Spirit. Paul's theology valued the mortal body as the temple of God's Spirit and anticipated a glorious metamorphosis of the body beyond physical death, parallel to the transformation of Jesus of Nazareth into the exalted Lord.

COMMUNICATING IN THE VERNACULAR

• Using a Bible dictionary, look up "Stoic" or "Stoicism," "Epicureanism," and "mystery religions" or "mystery." What more specific information do you find? With those ideas in mind, skim through several chapters of Romans or recall your insights from other chapters. Where and how do you see Paul using the vernacular to bolster or to communicate his gospel message?
• In what ways do we in the church attempt to use the vernacular to welcome or to communicate the gospel better to persons outside the church?
• How does "churchy" language or specific theological language affect your church's life? If, for example, this language communicates to a visitor that the church is only for the "insiders," how would the church know? What could be done to be more welcoming and open?

Paul's Letter to the Church at Rome and the Contemporary Church

Romans, Paul's longest and most thorough explanation of the Christian faith, did much to shape the beliefs and practices of Western civilization and of the Christian church around the world. Anyone hoping to provide leadership in the global village or hoping to develop an adequate Christian identity needs to be familiar with it. Next to the Synoptic Gospels, Romans is arguably the most important piece of Christian literature as a sourcebook of faith. Because it was written before the Gospels, it provides insights into the development of the Christian movement at its earliest stages. Since the circumstances that shaped the progress of Paul's mission from Antioch to Rome are in so many ways similar to and like a microcosm of today's global community, the pattern of church planting and evangelism that Paul employed can inform similar efforts today. The specific challenges and issues faced by the first missionary to the non-Jewish world were different than those to be faced in the 21st century. Nevertheless, a study of Paul's careful management of conflict and emphasis on life in the ✱ Spirit of Christ can set a pattern for similar pioneering efforts now. The diversity of culture and religion in the Roman Empire created a common vocabulary for communicating a new faith. So also, as Christians today enter into dialogue with people seeking vital spirituality but following a non-traditional path, a new language for creating fresh access to God for all persons may develop. Such openness and creativity requires maturity, confidence, powerful vision, and unwavering trust in the God who is beyond our words, symbols, understanding, or control. May the God whose mystery was revealed in the first century be made equally available to all people in the new millennium.

PAUL'S LETTER TO THE CHURCH AT ROME AND THE CONTEMPORARY CHURCH

• Summarize your learnings from Paul's closing remarks to the congregation at Rome. How does his obvious respect for and reliance on women and on a network of coworkers influence your view of Paul? of the church in his day? How are these insights useful in your attention to and work with the church and evangelistic practice today?

IN CLOSING

• Join together in prayer for the spread of the gospel today, particularly in areas that are oppressed or torn by violence and poverty. Pray for faithful men and women to take on the mantle of discipleship and for those who already risk their lives for this sacrificial ministry. In reflecting on the call of Jesus Christ to make disciples, take time in prayer if you wish to make or to reaffirm your own commitment to God.

---

[1] From "The Ecclesiastical Situation of the First Generation Roman Christians," by Andreas B. DuToit in *Hervormde Teologiese Studies* (Vol. 53, Summer, 1997); pages 498–512.
[2] From *Reading Romans*, by Luke Timothy Johnson (The Crossroad Publishing Company, 1997); page 220.